Advanced Introduction to Pr

Elgar Advanced Introductions are stimulating and thoughtful introductions to major fields in the social sciences and law, expertly written by the world's leading scholars. Designed to be accessible yet rigorous, they offer concise and lucid surveys of the substantive and policy issues associated with discrete subject areas.

The aims of the series are two-fold: to pinpoint essential principles of a particular field, and to offer insights that stimulate critical thinking. By distilling the vast and often technical corpus of information on the subject into a concise and meaningful form, the books serve as accessible introductions for undergraduate and graduate students coming to the subject for the first time. Importantly, they also develop well-informed, nuanced critiques of the field that will challenge and extend the understanding of advanced students, scholars and policy-makers.

For a full list of titles in the series please see the back of the book. Recent titles in the series include:

European Union Law
Jacques Ziller

Feminist Economics
Joyce P. Jacobsen

Planning Theory
Robert A. Beauregard

Tourism Destination Management
Chris Ryan

International Investment Law
August Reinisch

Sustainable Tourism
David Weaver

Austrian School of Economics
Second Edition
Randall G. Holcombe

U.S. Criminal Procedure
Christopher Slobogin

Platform Economics
Robin Mansell and W. Edward Steinmueller

Public Finance
Vito Tanzi

Human Dignity and Law
James R. May and Erin Daly

Space Law
Frans G. von der Dunk

Legal Research Methods
Ernst Hirsch Ballin

National Accounting
John M. Hartwick

Privacy Law
Megan Richardson

Advanced Introduction to

Privacy Law

MEGAN RICHARDSON

Professor of Law, Melbourne Law School, University of Melbourne, Australia

EE **Edward Elgar**
PUBLISHING

Cheltenham, UK • Northampton, MA, USA

Published by
Edward Elgar Publishing Limited
The Lypiatts
15 Lansdown Road
Cheltenham
Glos GL50 2JA
UK

Edward Elgar Publishing, Inc.
William Pratt House
9 Dewey Court
Northampton
Massachusetts 01060
USA

A catalogue record for this book
is available from the British Library

Library of Congress Control Number: 2020944311

ISBN 978 1 78897 094 5 (cased)
ISBN 978 1 78897 096 9 (paperback)
ISBN 978 1 78897 095 2 (eBook)

Typeset by Servis Filmsetting Ltd, Stockport, Cheshire

Printed and bound in Great Britain by TJ Books Limited, Padstow, Cornwall

Contents

Preface

'Privacy – do we have that now?' The question was put to me by an obviously sceptical immigration official as I entered the Netherlands in October 2018, on my way to the Amsterdam Privacy Conference. Despite my efforts at justifying my field in the next few seconds, I'm afraid not very articulately (in my defence I was coming off a flight from Melbourne), I was left with the impression that he remained unconvinced. I could understand the question – it is one I have often been asked in various guises over many years. There are so many reasons to think that despite our efforts at regulating for privacy in the current technological and social environment the law offers only marginal support for the boundaries and controls that individuals and groups seek to maintain. And especially now, in the midst of a pandemic where surveillance seems key to survival, we might wonder about the future of privacy given that, as philosopher Yuval Noah Harari says,[1] 'for the first time in human history, technology makes it possible to monitor everyone all the time'. On the other hand, much can be learnt from taking a longer view of the law's successful adaptations in the face of earlier new technologies and practices which have also challenged privacy. The insight is a starting point for this *Advanced Introduction to Privacy Law*.

This book falls within a genre of short books considering the state of privacy and privacy law in today's changing world. It is the kind of book I have been wanting to write for a very long time. I like to think of an advanced introduction as an intermediate form between simple reportage and the deeper analysis of a full monograph. Applied to privacy law, it offers an opportunity to reflect on the complex challenge of how to make space for privacy in the face of transformative technologies and the practices and norms they facilitate and foster. In the chapters that follow, the discussion ranges from the 15th century Gutenberg printing press, to photography, telegraph and telephone in

---

1   Yuval Noah Harari, 'The World After Coronavirus', *Financial Times* (London, 20 March 2020).

the 19th century, to television, computers and the internet beginning in the 20th century, to 21st century technologies of automation and artificial intelligence that may prove to be even more significant in their potential impact for human identity: our sense of self.

The manuscript for this book was largely finalised on 20 April 2020 (with a few updates added as it went to press). I am tremendously grateful to numerous friends, family members, colleagues and students who assisted me with finding material and formulating ideas over the years I have been working on privacy law. I especially thank Karin Clark, Mark Andrejevic and Beate Roessler for reading and commenting on sections of earlier drafts of the manuscript – although any errors, of course, are mine. Finally, my heartfelt appreciation to Luke Adams and Stephen Harries at Edward Elgar for enthusiastically encouraging me to write this book, accommodating my various deadline changes, and providing helpful advice at all stages of the process, and to Finn Halligan, Hetty Mosforth and Claire Banyard for meticulous and insightful editorial support.

1 Introduction

Should we even be thinking about privacy in the current age? In this book, I argue that we should, for all the ongoing and anticipated socio-technological challenges. Nevertheless, we need to acknowledge the scale of the challenges. The public internet with its architecture of open communication, underpinned and supported by digital technologies, certainly presents a special challenge to any idea that privacy can be maintained in the face of such a powerful force for transparency. And the implications of the digital context go well beyond the 'network of networks'.[1] Digital technologies shape devices and processes which rely on continuing accessibility to personal information, including of the most intimate kind, to carry out their functions. Their capacities for collection, storage, search, analysis, combination and dissemination of data of millions of people (or indeed just one or a few targeted persons or groups) give enormous power to those in a position to exercise control over the technologies *vis-à-vis* subjects. In short, we live in a 'global information society', where 'information technology governs virtually every aspect of our lives', as Justice Dr D Y Chandrachud observed in *Puttaswamy v Union of India* in 2017.[2] In these settings, it is not surprising to see the possibility of privacy becoming the subject of doubt, even while looking for ways to support it.

The doubt was there from the beginning. When John Perry Barlow proclaimed in the early 1990s that information 'wants to be free',[3] he was not just announcing the futility of intellectual property rights but of *any* laws that seek to restrain the spread of information. By 2012 Lawrence Lessig was saying that 'internet privacy' was an 'oxymoron' which only a redesign of the internet's architecture could overcome,

---

1 See William H Dutton, 'The Fifth Estate Emerging through the Network of Networks' (2009) 27 *Prometheus* 1.

2 *KS Puttaswamy v Union of India* (2017) 10 SCC 1.).

3 John Perry Barlow, 'The Economy of Ideas' (*Wired*, 1 March 1994) <https://www.wired.com/1994/03/economy-ideas>.

unlikely given the interests involved.[4] That was a year before former defence contractor Edward Snowden began to reveal the covert mass surveillance of individuals by governments working in tandem with telecommunications and internet companies. The revelations led to fresh concerns about the death of privacy. Another wave of concerns surfaced in the wake of the Cambridge Analytica-Facebook scandal in March 2018, focussed on data profiling of Facebook users through the Cambridge Analytica app allowed on the platform and exploited for political ends. London School of Economics student Srikanth Palle mused on his blog that Facebook might have to change its ways due to 'global outrage over the breach of user data on Facebook', but can we do without it?[5] Every time a new scandal breaks of private information kept for limited purposes being accessed, stored, handled, communicated and deployed in unexpected ways we hear arguments that the end of privacy has finally arrived.

Now added into the mix is the prospect of the intelligent machine designed and capable of shaping and carrying out its own automated decision-making processes based on patterns in the data (the raw material of information and knowledge), the subject of many anxious recent reports looking into the future of automation. Even without the extra element of artificial intelligence, automation is a hallmark of the current digital age – or as Tom Goodwin describes it, the 'post-digital age', when 'digital technology will be a vast, quiet element forming the seamless backbone of life', and 'the holders of data' will be 'the arbiters of mass behavioral change'.[6] And the question being debated is when will that come and how we will respond. As Yuval Noah Harari canvasses the issue, 'when mindless algorithms are able to teach, diagnose and design better than humans, what will we do?'[7] Indeed, what will we do when algorithms are simply cheaper and more scalable in carrying out these 'human-like' activities?[8] Is it too much also to say

---

4 Alex Fitzpatrick, 'Lawrence Lessig: Internet Privacy Is an Oxymoron' (*Mashable*, 21 June 2012) <https://mashable.com/2012/05/21/lessig-internet-privacy>.

5 Srikanth Palle, '"Privacy on the Internet? That's an Oxymoron" Facebook Data Scandal' (*Srikanth Economics*, 15 April 2018) <http://gyapy.com/view-article.php?aid=J4hoouQjvGwArDQV8im2V 2GxRVKCB51zgcDbqFdcz7U>.

6 Tom Goodwin, 'The Three Ages of Digital' (*TechCrunch*, 24 June 2016) <https://techcrunch.com/2016/06/23/the-three-ages-of-digital>.

7 Yuval Noah Harari, *Homo Deus: A Brief History of Tomorrow* (New York: HarperCollins 2017) 322.

8 Ajay Agrawal, Joshua Gans and Avi Goldfarb, *Prediction Machines: The Simple Economics of Artificial Intelligence* (Boston, Mass: HUP 2018).

of the powerful government and business interests pushing automation today that their purpose, and indeed their logic, is to take over all of our lives?[9] Or, as Shoshana Zuboff summarises the situation, 'it is no longer enough to automate information flows about us; the goal now is to automate us . . . and thus eliminate any possibility of self-determination'.[10]

Such reflections offer a very dystopian view of the possibilities of human freedom, identity and flourishing in the face of modern technologies. They also raise a set of concerns that seem to go beyond what we may call 'privacy' in its traditional sense of an imagined sphere 'of seclusion and protection from others (the public); of lack of accountability to "them"; and of related gains in closeness and comfort', as British cultural theorist Raymond Williams summarised things in the mid-1970s.[11] Or as Canadian sociologist Erving Goffman characterised it in the late 1950s, the distinction between the 'frontstage' (public) and 'backstage' (private) areas of life.[12] This traditional sense is still quite widely employed, with the ability to choose privacy in this sense treated as fundamental to human dignity and flourishing. But these days, 'privacy' is also quite often used (especially in the US) to denote control over personal information more broadly and to resist ubiquitous oppressive surveillance, enabled and aided by computerised technologies and practices. (We see a parallel language of 'data protection' in Europe.) Nevertheless, even these meanings may not quite capture the situation considered by Zuboff and others reflecting on threats to humanity posed by automated and AI systems.

Rather, what they seem to be signalling is the prospect of a debilitating control when human thoughts and behaviours are monitored and profiled relentlessly and on a massive scale, undermining our abilities

---

9 Shoshana Zuboff, *The Age of Surveillance Capitalism: The Fight for the Future at the New Frontier of Power* (New York: PublicAffairs 2019); Julie E Cohen, *Between Truth and Power: The Legal Constructions of Informational Capitalism*, (New York: OUP 2019); Mark Andrejevic, *Automated Media* (New York: Routledge 2020). See also Yuval Noah Harari, 'The World After Coronavirus', *Financial Times* (London, 20 March 2020).

10 Shoshana Zuboff interviewed by John Naughton, '"The Goal is to Automate us": Welcome to the Age of Surveillance Capitalism', *Guardian* (London, 20 January 2019).

11 Raymond Williams, *Keywords: A Vocabulary of Culture and Society* (London: Fontana 1976).

12 Erving Goffman, *The Presentation of Self in Everyday Life* (New York: Anchor 1959).

'to live rich, fulfilling lives',[13] to overcome inequalities,[14] to flourish in autonomous relationships,[15] and to participate as citizens in democratic processes.[16] The kinds of fears that George Orwell foreshadowed in his prophetic *Nineteen Eighty-Four* with its vision of an all-monitoring and thought-controlling Big Brother, watching the minutiae of human activity.[17]

1.1   Privacy under threat?

How far can the language of 'privacy' now be stretched to capture these fears? In 1949, Orwell was still talking about the end of 'private life', and hence privacy, as with the enhanced technology of television '[e]very citizen, or at least every citizen important enough to be worth watching, could be kept for twenty-four hours a day under the eyes of the police', adding that '[t]he possibility of enforcing not only complete obedience to the will of the State, but complete uniformity of opinion on all subjects, now existed'.[18] But, as Louis Menand writing in the *New Yorker* pertinently asks,[19] should we be thinking about a different vocabulary in our discussions of the dangers ahead? On the one hand, surveillance studies scholar David Lyon notes that issues have to do with digital society's monitory practices have tended to obviate older distinctions between private and public life.[20] In a similar vein, privacy scholars Mireille Hildebrandt and Bert-Jaap Koops suggest that

---

13 Ben Goold, 'Surveillance and the Political Value of Privacy' (2009) ALF 3, 4. And cf Cohen (n 9); Zuboff (n 9).

14 Mary Madden, Michele Gilman, Karen Levy and Alice Marwick, 'Privacy, Poverty, and Big Data: A Matrix of Vulnerabilities for Poor Americans' (2017) 95 *Wash U L Rev* 53; Anita Allen, *Unpopular Privacy: What Must We Hide?* (New York: Oxford 2017) ch 6; Khiara Bridges, *The Poverty of Privacy Rights* (Stanford, Cal: SUP 2017).

15 danah boyd and Alice Marwick, 'Social Privacy in Networked Publics: Teens' Attitudes, Practices, and Strategies' (Oxford Internet Institute *Decade in Internet Time* Symposium, 22 September 2011); Alice Marwick and danah boyd, 'Networked Privacy: How Teenagers Negotiate Context in Social Media' (2014) 16 *New Media & Soc* 1051; Sara Bannerman, 'Relational Privacy and the Networked Governance of the Self' (2019) 22 *Inf Commun Soc* 2187.

16 Goold (n 13); Neil Richards, 'The Dangers of Surveillance' (2013) 126 *Harv L Rev* 1934; Andrew Roberts, 'A Republican Account of the Value of Privacy' (2015) 14 *Eur J Pol Theor* 320.

17 George Orwell, *Nineteen Eighty-Four* (London: Secker & Warburg 1949; New York: Harcourt, Brace & Co 1949).

18 ibid ch 9.

19 Louis Menand, 'Why Do We Care So Much About Privacy?', *New Yorker* (New York, 11 June 2018).

20 David Lyon, *The Culture of Surveillance: Watching as a Way of Life* (Cambridge, UK: Polity 2018) 32–33.

'privacy', at least conventionally understood, is a dated concept in the face of the major challenges we now face.[21] Nevertheless, many privacy scholars seem content to use an ever-expanding language of 'privacy' to talk about new threats. But Zuboff takes a different position, arguing that although we rely on categories such as 'privacy', 'the existing categories nevertheless fall short in identifying and contesting the most crucial and unprecedented facts of this new regime'.[22]

I am inclined to agree with Zuboff (and Menand) that it would be nice to see a new vocabulary, moving beyond the discourse of privacy in talking about issues which have more broadly to do with the exercise of control over human identity in our increasingly digitalised and automated society – even if, for now, the language of privacy works well enough to capture this idea. At the same time, I want to suggest that the older idea about privacy as concerned with maintaining a private sphere can still play a useful role even in a more modern environment, despite its greater blurring between public and private. I find support for this position in a 2011 ethnographical study of danah boyd and Alice Marwick looking at practices of young people using social networks with users becoming actively engaged in sharing intimate details of their lives online.[23] Interestingly boyd and Marwick found that participants worked hard to maintain boundaries around what they considered to be their private lives, even 'in public', and insisted that sharing online does not mean sharing with everyone – adapting their techniques to protect their ideas of private life to accommodate the porousness of the digital environment. Indeed, even Mark Zuckerberg of Facebook has recently noted that 'many people prefer the intimacy of communicating one-on-one with just a few friends', preferring the privacy of the living room to the town square, and adding that social media platforms such as Facebook need to adapt to support that choice.[24] While many may doubt whether Zuckerberg is the best person to be talking about privacy given Facebook's record of failures, he makes an important point about continuing human preferences for the intimacy of private life – and further, that rather than being employed to undermine boundaries between private and public

---

21 Mireille Hildebrandt and Bert-Jaap Koops, 'The Challenges of Ambient Law and Legal Protection in the Profiling Era' (2010) 73 *MLR* 428.

22 Zuboff (n 9) 14.

23 boyd and Marwick (n 15); Marwick and boyd (n 15).

24 Mark Zuckerberg, 'A Privacy-Focussed Vision for Social Networking' (Facebook, 6 March 2019) <https://www.facebook.com/notes/mark-zuckerberg/a-privacy-focused-vision-for-social-networking/10156700570096634>.

life, technology and practices should ideally be designed to support them. This reminds me of visionary Australian urban designer William Mitchell in the early 2000s, writing about everyday life in a future hyper-connected digital world, observing that '[s]ometimes we want to be private; sometimes we want to put ourselves on display' – adding 'what's required are sophisticated systems that are able to control the level of public visibility [we have] at any moment'.[25] Rather than imagining a future where private life is ceded to the power of ubiquitous technologies and practices, Mitchell was imagining that scope for privacy could be maintained and even built into the systems which could be operated under our control.

1.2   New/old debates

Of course, debates about the effects of new technologies and practices for privacy and identity stretch back well beyond the last 30 years even if their precise starting point is a matter of some debate and discussion.[26] In the 18th century concerns about the privacy of prisoners potentially subject to Jeremy Bentham's proposed 'Panopticon' prison, with its technology of ubiquitous overlooking by unseen guards,[27] may have been muted – and it was really only in the 20th century that the Panopticon was to become a significant reference point for discussions of totalitarian policing.[28] Likewise, we see embryonic language of privacy in the 1765 case of *Entick v Carrington*,[29] where journalist John Entick objected to his premises being searched without proper warrant by agents of the Earl of Halifax, looking for evidence of sedition, arguing trespass to property Lord Camden's rhetoric in this case formed the basis of the prohibition on unreasonable search and seizure in the US Constitution's Fourth Amendment. Some noted scholars have argued that *Entick* was as close as one could get to a case about

25 Victor Chase, 'Why Buck Rogers Will Be Invisible: Interview with William J Mitchell', *Pictures of the Future* (Spring 2004) 34 <https://www.docme.ru/doc/86920>.

26 See Megan Richardson, *The Right to Privacy: Origins and Influence of a Nineteenth-Century Idea* (Cambridge, UK: CUP 2017); Michael Tugendhat, *Liberty Intact: Human Rights in English Law* (Oxford, UK: OUP 2017) ch 10.

27 Jeremy Bentham, *Panopticon; or, The Inspection House* (first published 1791) in John Bowring (ed), *Works of Jeremy Bentham* (Edinburgh: William Tait 1843) vol 4, 40.

28 See David Rosen and Aaron Santesso, 'The Panopticon Reviewed: Sentimentalism and Eighteenth-Century Interiority' (2010) 77 *ELH* 1041.

29 *Entick v Carrington* (1765) 19 St Tr 1029.

the right to privacy in this time of limited 'privacy' legal thinking.[30] Nevertheless, by the 19th century the language of a right to privacy was clearly evident and we see this reflected in the legal discourse, including in cases concerning unwanted publications of private letters and private images facilitated by new print technologies and a media environment of proliferating newspapers and magazines and circulating photographs. And, by 1890, in a famous article in the *Harvard Law Review*,[31] Samuel Warren and Louis Brandeis identified 'instantaneous photographs and newspaper enterprise' as major threats to the privacy of private life in modern America, arguing that the right to be 'let alone' in the face of these modern technologies and practices of intrusion should now be identified and protected as a right of 'inviolate personality'.

Nor was this the end of the matter. By 1928, Brandeis J, by now an Associate Justice of the US Supreme Court, was raising powerful concerns about the implications of telephone tapping practices employed by the state in the name of policing and security in prohibition-era *Olmstead v United States*,[32] citing *Entick v Carrington* along with his article with Warren and presciently warning that newer technologies would allow even greater 'intrusion' into 'the most intimate occurrences of the home', and insidious 'means of exploring unexpressed, beliefs, thoughts and emotions'. While in *Olmstead* Justice Brandeis was dissenting, his position was eventually to become the Supreme Court's position, treating the Fourth Amendment as embodying a constitutional 'right to privacy' *vis-à-vis* the state. In Europe, with the experience of powerful bureaucratic regimes and technical systems portrayed in alarming terms in the works of Max Weber and Franz Kafka, new thinking about how to establish and maintain data protection standards was starting to develop[33] – offering a response to sociologist Georg Simmel's point that the 'deepest problems of modern life' derive from efforts of individuals to maintain 'independence and individuality' in the face of 'the sovereign power of society ... [and the weight of] the external culture and technique of life'.[34] And so ideas about the challenges of modern life circulating at the beginning of

---

30 See, for instance, Tugendhat (n 26).

31 Samuel D Warren and Louis D Brandeis, 'The Right to Privacy' (1890) 4 *Harv L Rev* 193, 215.

32 *Olmstead v United States*, 277 US 438, 474 (1928), Brandeis J dissenting.

33 See Malcolm Warner, 'Kafka, Weber and Organization Theory' (2007) 60 *Human Relations* 1019.

34 Georg Simmel, 'The Metropolis and Mental Life' (1903), in Edward A Shils (transl, ed with Donald N Levine), *On Individuality and Social Forms* (Chicago, Ill: U of Chicago Press 1971) 324.

the 20th century helped to shape European ideas about the need to regulate for private life and data protection later in the century. As well, there was the experience of endemic disregard of human rights, the right to privacy included, during World War II and the continuing threats posed by post-war totalitarian regimes, including the Stalinist Soviet Union which Orwell was already writing about in *Nineteen Eighty-Four*, published in 1949.[35] It can certainly be said that the war-time experience was a major factor in setting in train the post-war human rights systems which provided *inter alia* for the right to privacy so resoundingly, and the arguments for the right to privacy continued to grow and develop afterwards.

Much of the thinking of the post-war period was directed not just at the obvious totalitarian regimes. For instance, Australian jurist Sir Zelman Cowen in 1969 warned that 'our political masters demand of us an ever-growing accounting of our lives and affairs', in this language invoking a fearsome image of Orwell's 'Big Brother'.[36] Around the same time in the US, political scientist and legal scholar Alan Westin was detailing serious concerns about the prospects of computerised data-bases being used by governments and organisations to store personal data for dubious or unknown purposes and technologies of surveil-lance being deployed indiscriminately against individuals and groups.[37] Westin was arguing for expanded legal protection of privacy (broadly construed) in the face of these challenges. But by the end of the cen-tury, some notable scholars were expressing serious doubts about the possibility of privacy from the subject's point of view, given the evi-dent human responses to the new media technologies and practices permeating everyday life – as, for example, with Italian philosopher Umberto Eco's comment in 2000 that the popular television program 'Big Brother' had created and exploited a situation where 'some indi-viduals decide freely (if misguidedly) to let themselves be spied on by a mass audience, which is happy to do the spying', suggesting that a 'col-lapse in boundaries' was leading to the 'paradoxical' situation where, despite all the laws enacted to protect privacy, people 'struggle for a defence of privacy in a society of exhibitionists'.[38] Compare here Lyon's

---

35 Orwell (n 17).

36 Sir Zelman Cowen, *The Private Man* (Boyer Lectures, Sydney: ABC 1969) 5.

37 Alan F Westin, *Privacy and Freedom* (New York: Atheneum 1967).

38 Umberto Eco, 'The Loss of Privacy', conference organised by Stefano Rodotà (Venice, September 2000), in *Turning Back the Clock: Hot Wars and Media Populism* (transl Alistair McEwen, Orlando, Fla: Harcourt 2007) 77, 79–82.

suggestion in 2018 that we are becoming inured to the prospect of ubiquitous surveillance and indeed 'willing' participants in the digital society's monitory practices.[39]

Nevertheless, even in the face of what appears to be a quite reasonable pessimism about the future of privacy, I want to argue that space for privacy can be found in the present and future as in the past, supported effectively by law. The main task will be how to refashion law as a sufficiently sophisticated system of its own, responding to the powerful and sophisticated technologies and practices (and sometimes even social norms) on the other side.

1.3   Approach of this book

It is a tremendous challenge to write a short book that gives an overview of privacy law, takes account of a rich and expanding literature, and offers insights into future directions along with some ideas about how the law should ideally be fashioned for the protection of privacy (while not losing sight of other important rights, freedoms and interests which we also want to see protected).[40] Fortunately, there are others who have taken on the challenge , including Raymond Wacks in his now classic *Privacy: A Very Short Introduction* published by Oxford University Press and currently in its second edition,[41] Daniel Solove and Paul Schwartz's *Privacy Law Fundamentals*, with a rich array of summaries of legislation and cases along with references to key literature,[42] and political theorist Annabelle Lever's insightful *On Privacy*, published by Routledge.[43] Reference can also be made to some useful introductory chapters in larger works,[44] as well as larger

---

39 Lyon (n 20).

40 As to which, see Soumitra Dutta, William S Dutton and Ginette Law, *The New Internet World: A Global Perspective on Freedom of Expression, Privacy, Trust and Security Online* (INSEAD Faculty & Research Working Paper, 2011).

41 Raymond Wacks, *Privacy: A Very Short Introduction*, 2nd edn (Oxford, UK: OUP 2015).

42 Daniel J Solove and Paul M Schwartz, *Privacy Law Fundamentals* (Portsmouth, NH: International Association of Privacy Professionals 2013). See also Daniel J Solove, 'A Brief History of Information Privacy Law' in Kristen Mathews (ed), *Proskauer on Privacy: A Guide to Privacy and Data Security Law in the Information Age*, 2nd edn (Practising Law Institute 2017) ch 1.

43 Annabelle Lever, *On Privacy* (New York: Routledge 2012).

44 For instance, Gavin Phillipson, 'Press Freedom, the Public Interest and Privacy' in Andrew T Kenyon (ed), *Comparative Defamation and Privacy Law* (Cambridge, UK: CUP 2016) ch 8; Jan Oster, *Media Freedom as a Fundamental Right* (Cambridge, UK: CUP 2015) ch 7; Jacob Rowbottom, *Media Law* (Oxford, UK: Hart 2018) ch 2; Marc A Franklin, David A Anderson,

works on privacy law providing key information and further references.[45] And there are now many excellent online sources including, on the academic side, the collaborative Inforrm's blog,[46] Daniel Solove's TeachPrivacy blog,[47] and Graham Greenleaf's Web Pages.[48]

That said, I do not seek to cover the ground in quite the same way as these other introductory texts. My interest is how law adapts in response to contextual changes – and how it might continue to adapt in the future. In the next chapter, I review the meaning and value of 'privacy', a term which itself has adapted in meaning somewhat to accommodate the changing circumstances of the industrial and now digital age. In the chapters following, I move on to examine the ways in which 'the right to privacy' has also been identified and supported as a matter of law, and not just because of its identification as a human right in post-war declarations and conventions beginning with the United Nations' Universal Declaration of Human Rights in 1948,[49] the Council of Europe's European Convention on Human Rights in 1950,[50] and the European Union's Charter of Fundamental Rights 2000, where the right to 'private and family life' is supplemented with a right to data protection.[51] At the ground level, legislative regimes such as the EU General Data Protection Regulation 2016 (drawing on the right to data protection in the EU Charter) and California Consumer Privacy Act 2018[52] provide for a range of rights and obligations tailored to the data processing practices of a digital age, supplementing other legal protections. In the final chapter, I return to the question of whether the right to privacy will continue to play an important role in addressing the transformations we are experiencing, whether in its original or somewhat different form, and how that might play out in legal terms specifically. In short, the question is whether a right to privacy that 'we

Lyrissa C Barnett Lidsky and Amy Gajda, *Media Law: Cases and Materials*, 9th edn (St Paul, Minn: Foundation Press 2019) ch 5.

45 For instance, Tanya Aplin, Lionel Bently, Phillip Johnson, Simon Malynicz, *Gurry on Breach of Confidence: The Protection of Confidential Information* (Oxford, UK: OUP 2012); NA Moreham and Sir Mark Warby (Sir Michael Tugendhat and Iain Christie consultant eds), *Tugendhat and Christie: The Law of Privacy and the Media*, 3rd edn (Oxford, UK: OUP 2016); Daniel J Solove and Paul M Schwartz, *Information Privacy Law*, 6th edn (Wolters Kluwer 2017).

46 Inforrm's Blog: The International Forum for Responsible Media Blog <https://inforrm.org>.

47 TeachPrivacy privacy + security blog <https://teachprivacy.com/privacy-security-training-blog>.

48 Graham Greenleaf's Web Pages <http://www2.austlii.edu.au/~graham>.

49 Universal Declaration of Human Rights, United Nations General Assembly 1948, Art 12.

50 European Convention on Human Rights, Council of Europe 1950, Art 8.

51 Charter of Fundamental Rights of the European Union 2000, Arts 7 and 8.

52 *General Data Protection Regulation* (EU) 2016/679.

have inherited from the past', as Lever puts it,[53] can assist in addressing complex questions of how to protect the human condition in centuries to come. While I am hopeful that individuals and groups will continue to see the value of privacy, and that laws in many jurisdictions will find ways to support this, I end on a note of speculation. In other words, my argument is that law *can* effectively regulate for privacy – not that it necessarily *will*. And, although there are a number of intriguing positive signs in the latest developments, there are also some new challenges ahead as I finish this book in the midst of a major terrifying pandemic where a major priority is basically one of saving lives.

What I am offering is only a brief look at some very complex and troublesome questions about the state of privacy and privacy law in the current environment. Some may consider it too brief. Certainly, more can be said about the relations between the past, present and future of ideas such as 'the right to privacy' which now seem firmly embedded in law but were once quite novel[54] – and already some interesting new revisionist accounts are emerging.[55] For now, though, my modest aim with this *Advanced Introduction to Privacy Law* is to provide a snapshot of privacy as a constantly evolving modern social phenomenon along with its legal implications.

---

53 Lever (n 43) 1–2.

54 As to which, see Megan Richardson, *The Right to Privacy: Origins and Influence of a Nineteenth-Century Idea* (Cambridge, UK: CUP 2017); Beate Roessler, 'Privacy as a Human Right' (2017) 117 *Proc Aristot Soc* 187.

55 See, for instance, Jessica Lake, *The Face that Launched a Thousand Lawsuits: The American Women Who Forged A Right To Privacy* (New Haven, Conn: YUP 2016); Jennifer Rothman, *The Right of Publicity: Privacy Reimagined for a Public World* (Cambridge, Mass: HUP 2018); Sarah E Igo, *The Known Citizen: A History of Privacy in Modern America* (Cambridge, Mass: HUP 2018); Andrea Monti and Raymond Wacks, *The Right to Privacy Reconsidered* (Oxford, UK: Hart 2019); Jake Goldenfein, *Monitoring Laws: Profiling and Identity in the World State* (New York: CUP 2020).

2   Meaning and value of privacy

A great deal of philosophical and legal debate about privacy concerns its meaning and value. As a philosopher, Annabelle Lever is one of those who have observed this. However, she also notes that the level of definitional controversy is surprising, as 'it is doubtful that privacy really is any harder to define than any other complex right or value'.[1] In this chapter, I explore the reasons for the special complexity associated with privacy. I suggest that one reason may be the relatively recent status of the right to privacy (at least as far as law is concerned), with the result that it remains a less well-established and thus more contestable right compared with other rights of more ancient lineage, such as the right to free speech and the right to property which are now well-entrenched even if they are still much debated. Further, another reason may be that the meaning of 'privacy' seems to have undergone a process of revision over recent decades in response to pressures for expanded coverage of the right to privacy to address current challenges. Yet it is important to acknowledge that the right to privacy – or to 'private life' to use the older expression that was popular for much of its history,[2] comparable to the French *la vie privée* – is still importantly, as Lever says, a right 'inherited from the past'.[3] Likewise, when it comes to assessing its meaning, bearing in mind Ferdinand de Saussure's observation that language 'always appears as a heritage of the previous period',[4] we can still see the powerful residue of an older historical meaning even in more modern discussions.

---

1 Annabelle Lever, *On Privacy* (New York: Routledge 2012) 3.

2 See Google Ngram Viewer <https://books.google.com/ngrams> (search for 'privacy' and 'private life).

3 Lever (n 1) 1–2.

4 Ferdinand de Saussure, *Course in General Linguistics*, Charles Bally and Albert Sechehaye with Albert Reidlinger (eds) (first published Paris: Payot 1916, Wade Baskin tr, London: Peter Owen 1960) 67, 71.

2.1   Protecting private life

Online Etymology Dictionary suggests that 'privacy' came to mean 'freedom from intrusion' around the beginning of the 19th century.[5] This was a period associated with Romantic themes of emotion, imagination and creativity, the individual and close community – especially in the Western world, but with parallels in the East and South, reflecting what Michael Franklin describes as a 'two-way process of transculturation'.[6] Some may question whether the early 19th century was the starting point of this meaning, pointing to a longer history of an intimate private sphere developing alongside the Habermasian public sphere spurred on by the Gutenberg press.[7] And they may bolster this with evidence of practices of private reading and quiet conversations developing in late-18th century London coffeehouses – part and parcel of the general shift taking place from Enlightenment to early Romanticism in that period.[8] But we can say that privacy at least by the 19th century carried a signification of a sphere of private life that those fortunate enough to be able to choose (ie, with sufficient resources and influence) felt entitled to choose, designating it as off-limits, non-intrudable, free from the public gaze. As George Crabb put it in his popular *English Synonyms* in 1816, '*Privacy* is opposed to publicity: he who lives in *privacy*, therefore, is one who follows no public line, who lives so as to be little known.'[9]

The meaning was evident in Jane Austen's *Mansfield Park* published in 1814,[10] just two years earlier than Crabb's *English Synonyms* and four years before the case of *Gee v Pritchard*,[11] where the privacy of private letters sent between family members, stepmother and stepson who might almost have come out of one of Austen's novels, was the subject of express discussion. In that case Lord Eldon concluded

5   *Online Etymology Dictionary* (*Etymonline*) <https://www.etymonline.com> (etymology of 'privacy').

6   Michael J Franklin, 'General Introduction and [Meta]Historical Background [Re]Presenting the Palanquins of State; Or, *Broken Leaves in a Mughal Garden*' in Michael J Franklin (ed), *Romantic Representations of British India* (London & New York: Routledge 2006) 1, 18.

7   Jürgen Habermas, *The Structural Formation of the Public Sphere* (Berlin: Hermann Luchterhand Verlag 1962 (Thomas Burger with Frederick Lawrence tr, Cambridge, Mass: MIT Press 1989).

8   See Brian Cowan, 'Publicity and Privacy in the History of the British Coffeehouse' (2007) 5 *Hist Compass* 1180.

9   George Crabb, *English Synonyms Explained in Alphabetical Order* (London: printed for Baldwin, Cradock & Joy 1816) 675

10 Jane Austen, *Mansfield Park* (Whitehall, London: T Egerton 1814).

11 *Gee v Pritchard* (1818) 2 Swans 402.

that adequate protection against the defendant's intended publication could be found in the common law property right in published works (subsequently subsumed under copyright), adding that 'I do not say that I am to interfere because the letters are written in confidence, or because the publication of them may wound the feelings of the Plaintiff; but if mischievous effects of that kind can be apprehended in cases in which this Court has been accustomed, on the ground of property, to forbid publication, it would not become me to abandon the jurisdiction which my predecessors have exercised, and refuse to forbid it'.[12] Likewise, in this early novel focussed on family relations and friendship Austen examines the distress that may be wrought through a breach of the boundaries of private and domestic life with unusual attention. In one notable scene fairly early on in the book , Austen's character Edmund Bertram, in talking to Fanny Price, juxtaposes 'privacy and propriety' of interactions between trusted intimates engaged in a private family theatrical production against 'the excessive intimacy' of having an outsider thrust into the family circle, brought into the production by one of the family members, and able to observe and comment on the proceedings at will.[13] Thus, we have the idea of a desirable proper intimacy bestowed on selected private friends and families at will, as distinct from an 'excessive intimacy' imposed with unwanted outsiders.

It was an idea that would reverberate in literary fictions of the 19th century, especially as penned by women (authorities on domestic space), involving scenes of felicitous domestic privacy. A typical example, noted by Katherine Adams in her fascinating account of *Privacy, Property and Belonging in US Women's Life Writings, 1840–1890*,[14] is Louisa May Alcott's *Little Women*, and its sequels published between 1868 and 1886,[15] where the female protagonist Jo Bhaer nee Marsh (and the alter ego of the book's famous Author) finds the professional literary success she so desires for her writing but despairs at her loss of liberty in the face of her determined fans, preferring 'the privacy of her home to the pedestal on which she was requested to pose'.[16]

---

12 ibid 426.
13 Austen (n 10) vol 1, 321.
14 Katherine Adams, *Owning Up: Privacy, Property, and Belonging in US Women's Life Writing, 1840–1890* (Oxford, UK: OUP 2009) ch 5.
15 Louisa M Alcott, *Little Women* (Boston, US: Roberts Brothers 1868); *Little Men* (Boston, Mass: Roberts Brothers 1871); Louisa M Alcott, *Jo's Boys, And How They Turned Out: A Sequel to 'Little Men'* (Boston, Mass: Roberts Brothers 1886).
16 Alcott, *Jo's Boys* (n 15) ch 3.

Contrast such narratives with Daniel Defoe's *Robinson Crusoe*, published a century before *Mansfield Park*. At the beginning of his fictional
autobiographical account of his experience of being marooned on a
desert island, Crusoe rails against his 'Affliction' of 'being banished
from human Society, . . . alone, circumscribed from the boundless
Ocean, cut off from Man', only later coming to experience some pleas-
ure in new domestic and friendship alliances, enjoying the security of
a cave retreat on the most retired parts of the island, and appreciating
'the Wisdom of Providence' he accrues through his adventures.[17] Thus
arguably in 1719 we already have an embryonic sense of benefits to
be gained from a private and domestic existence, softening the earlier
impression that in Crusoe's world, the state of being private may easily
be associated with an undesirable banishment, or imposed solitude.
But the value of privacy was still being learned in Defoe's time –
another step in what French privacy historian Philippe Ariès refers to
as the changes taking place 'in material and spiritual life, in relations
between the individual and state, and in the family' in the Modern Age
ushered in by the Gutenberg press, 'even bearing in mind all that is
owed to the Middle Ages (seen of course in a new light)'.[18] It may have
been more conventional by Austen's time in 1814 (and certainly was by
Alcott's time). And by 1819 French philosopher-politician Pierre-Paul
Royer-Collard could proclaim that 'private life must be walled off!' as a
self-evident aspiration for free citizens of the Republic.[19] But for much
of the 18th century public understandings of privacy and its value were
still quite rudimentary, as shown by Samuel Johnson's 1755 *Dictionary
of the English Language*, identifying privacy in terms of solitude and
secrecy without reference to the enjoyment of private life within the
walls.[20]

Nevertheless, just ten years later, in the case of *Entick v Carrington*
in 1765 we see a glimmer of the interior as well as exterior character
of privacy, albeit still quite embryonic. Radical journalist John Entick

---

17 [Daniel Defoe], *The Life and Strange Surprising Adventures of Robinson Crusoe, Mariner* (printed
    for the Book-Sellers of London and Westminster 1719).
18 Philippe Ariès, 'Introduction' in Philippe Ariès and Georges Duby (eds), *A History of Private Life*,
    vol 3: *Passions of the Renaissance* (Cambridge, Mass: Belknap Press 1989) 2.
19 M de Barante, *La Vie Politique de M Royer-Collard, ses discours et ses ecrits*, 2nd edn (Paris: Didier
    1861) 474–75.
20 Samuel Johnson, *A Dictionary of the English Language: In which the words are deduced from their
    originals, and illustrated in their different significations by examples from the best writers* (London:
    printed by W Strahan, for J and P Knapton; T and T Longman; C Hitch and L Hawes; A Millar;
    and R and J Dodsley 1755) (definition of 'privacy').

objected to emissaries of the state entering his house without proper warrant searching for evidence of sedition, remaining there for four hours disturbing him in his peaceful possession, who searched and examined the rooms, breaking open the locks on the boxes, and 'read over, pried into, and examined all the private papers, books, &c of the plaintiff there found, whereby the secret affairs, &c of the plaintiff became wrongfully discovered and made public'.[21] Lord Camden responded that private papers are among a person's 'dearest possessions', and where these are removed and carried away, 'the secret nature of those goods will be an aggravation of the trespass'.[22] In legal terms the case was simply one of common law trespass to private property, although now some notable scholars including retired judge Michael Tugendhat in *Liberty Intact: Human Rights in English Law*, consider it an important early (or precursor) case about privacy of private property *vis-à-vis* the state especially.[23] And in the US it formed the backdrop of the Fourth Amendment's prohibition on unreasonable searches and seizures, later characterised as a Constitutional right to privacy.[24] Over the course of this history, understandings of privacy have also become richer, as in *Olmstead v United States* in 1928, where Justice Brandeis (in a position later endorsed by the Supreme Court) argued that unwarranted telephone tapping was an invasion of a suspect's Fourth Amendment right, warning that newer technologies would allow even greater 'intrusion' into 'the most intimate occurrences of the home', and insidious 'means of exploring unexpressed, beliefs, thoughts and emotions'.[25]

What we see, then, in these cases, is a growing association of 'privacy' with protection from intrusion with a parallel conception of a valuable 'private life', lying within the walls. 'Private life', or '*la vie privée*' to use the equivalent French expression, was coming to represent a private sphere associated with intimacy and domesticity sheltered from various kinds of intrusion facilitated by the new communications technologies and practices of the long 19th century. The same can be seen in other cases concerning intrusions not just by agents of the

---

21 *Entick v Carrington* (1765) 19 St Tr 1029.

22 ibid 1066.

23 See, for instance, Michael Tugendhat, *Liberty Intact: Human Rights in English Law* (Oxford, UK: OUP 2017) ch 10.

24 See *Boyd v United States*, 116 US 616 (1886); *Olmstead v United States*, 277 US 438 (1928), Brandeis J dissenting; *Katz v United States* 389 US 347 (1967); *Carpenter v United States*, 585 US– (2018); 138 S Ct 2206.

25 *Olmstead v United States* (n 24) 473–74 (Brandeis J dissenting).

state, as in *Entick* and *Olmstead*, but also by other instrumentalities of society, including the media, (other) business enterprise, as well as certain individuals, which were also proliferating.[26] For instance, in *Félix c O'Connell* decided by the Tribunal de la Seine in Paris in 1858, an artist's unauthorised circulation of a deathbed image based on a photograph made for the family of the French actress Mme Élisa Rachel Félix was characterised as a breach of the domestic intimacy that the family should be able to enjoy in peace.[27] A decade earlier in London, in the 'royal etchings' case of *Prince Albert v Strange* in 1849 – surely the leading English privacy case of the 19th century – the language of the right to privacy was used by Lord Cottenham to denote the royal couple's right to prevent a public exhibition of their domestic etchings which had come into the defendant's hands most likely through the agency of a printer or his assistant given the plates for the purpose of making limited copies for circulation to family and friends,[28] drawing on the equitable doctrine of breach of confidence and the common law property right in unpublished works discussed in *Gee v Pritchard* in 1818. Nor was thinking about domestic privacy limited to the Western world. In 1888, in the Indian case of *Gokal Prasad v Radho*[29] judges talked of the physical separation of women within the home under Parda as a social custom embedded in Hindu and Muslim culture requiring a legal response against a neighbour's overlooking in aid of what Justice Mahmood called the 'immemorial right of privacy', and the Chief Justice, Sir John Edge, referred to as 'the comfort and value' of the home. Just two years later, Samuel Warren and Louis Brandeis's article on 'The Right to Privacy' was published in the *Harvard Law Review* in 1890. We see the influence of the 19th century on these authors' arguments that the law should recognise more fully the right to be 'let alone', guarding against 'intrusion upon the domestic circle' and 'protect[ing] the privacy of private life'.[30] In their language of the right to privacy as a right to be let alone, a right to be free from intrusion into private life, these authors reflected the Saussurian logic that the meaning of a sign is determined by the understanding of the community.[31]

---

26 See Megan Richardson, *The Right to Privacy: Origins and Influence of a Nineteenth-Century Idea* (Cambridge, UK: CUP 2017).

27 *Félix v O'Connell*, 1858, Trib civ de la Seine (1ere Ch, *Dalloz* 1858) 3.

28 *Prince Albert v Strange* (1849) 1 H & Tw 1.

29 *Gokal Prasad v Radho* (1888) ILR 10 Allahabad 358.

30 Samuel D Warren and Louis D Brandeis, 'The Right to Privacy' (1890) 4 *Harv L Rev* 193, 195, 205, 215.

31 Saussure (n 4) 67, 71.

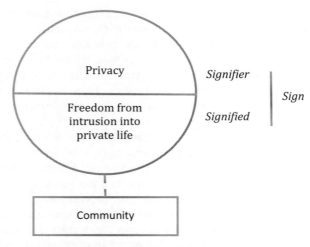

Figure 2.1   Privacy as freedom from intrusion into private life (circa 1890)

2.2   A growing sense of right

So what was the character of this 'right'? Was it just a matter of a current social norm rooted in the particular social conditions of time and place? Or was there more to it? There is a hint at its social normative status in Warren and Brandeis's suggestion, writing at the end of the 19th century, that by now the older right to life could generally be understood as encompassing a right to 'enjoy life' as an incident of the '[t]he intense intellectual and emotional life, and the heightening of sensations which came with the advance of civilization'.[32] But they also posited a deeper moral basis in their identification of the right as a right of 'inviolate personality',[33] using a Kantian digitarian rhetoric. At the same time, their reference to privacy as an aspect of a right to 'enjoy life' gestures to 19th century liberal-utilitarian ideas about human flourishing – evident, for instance, in American philosopher Ralph Waldo Emerson's advocation of individual resistance to conformity *Self-Reliance* published in 1841,[34] and in English liberal utilitarian philosopher John Stuart

---

32 Warren and Brandeis (n 30) 193.

33 ibid 205.

34 Ralph Waldo Emerson, 'Self-Reliance' (first published 1841, Ronald A Bosco and Joel Myerson (eds), *Ralph Waldo Emerson: The Major Prose* (Cambridge, Mass: Belknap 2015)) 127.

Mill's arguments for liberty as crucial to human flourishing and social progress in *On Liberty*, published in 1859.[35] And, although Mill, like other utilitarians of the 19th century, resisted the 18th century Blackstonian idea of there being natural rights based on natural law (famously dismissed by Jeremy Bentham as 'nonsense upon stilts'),[36] he acknowledged that in the discourse of 'rights' there is a sense of these being 'vital to human well-being', a matter of 'indispensable . . . necess[ity]', 'making safe for us the groundwork of our existence': thus '[t]he claim assumes the character of absoluteness, that apparent infinity, and incommensurability with all other considerations, which constitute the distinction between the feeling of right and wrong and that of ordinary expediency and inexpediency . . . and recognised indispensability becomes a moral necessity, analogous to physical, and often not inferior to it in binding force'.[37] (As such, Mill's reasoning based on utilitarian considerations fitted with what Bentham was prepared to allow as a legitimate statement of moral claim, appealing to the principle of utility.)[38]

In subsequent centuries, the right to privacy conceived as a right to freedom from intrusion into private life,[39] variously characterised as a right of in-access,[40] of non-transparency,[41] of boundary-setting,[42] or in more positive terms a right to enjoy a 'sphere of intimate and domestic life',[43] with a particular focus on 'intimate information' (at least some are inclined to suggest),[44] has been argued for by many dignitarian and liberal thinkers, along with some utilitarians, as a basic human right. And while often instrumental in other rights and freedoms going to safety and belonging, knowledge and understanding,

---

35 John Stuart Mill, 'On Liberty' (first published 1859) in Mary Warnock (ed), *Utilitarianism, On Liberty, Essay on Bentham* (London: Collins 1962) 126, 138 and ch 3.

36 See Jeremy Bentham, 'Anarchical Fallacies; Being an Examination of the Declarations of Rights issued during the French Revolution' (first published 1792) in John Bowring (ed), *Works of Jeremy Bentham* (Edinburgh: William Tait 1843) vol 2, 489.

37 Mill, 'Utilitarianism' (first published 1861) in Warnock (n 35), ch 5, 311–17.

38 Philip Schofield, 'Jeremy Bentham's "Nonsense upon Stilts"' (2003) 15 *Utilitas* 1.

39 cf *Douglas v Hello! Ltd* [2001] QB 967, Sedley LJ at [126] ('unwanted intrusion into their personal lives').

40 Ruth Gavison, 'Privacy and the Limits of Law' (1980) 89 *Yale LJ* 421, 423.

41 Lisa Austin, 'Privacy and the Question of Technology' (2003) 22 *Law & Phil* 119.

42 Kirsty Hughes, 'A Behavioural Understanding of Privacy and its Implications for Privacy Law' (2012) 75 *MLR* 806.

43 'More Data, More Problems': Developments in the Law (2018) 131 *Harv L Rev* 1714, 1766.

44 See Charles Fried, 'Privacy' (1968) 77 *Yale LJ* 475, 484; Andrea Monti and Raymond Wacks, *The Right to Privacy Reconsidered* (Oxford, UK: Hart 2019).

and political participation in democratic institutions, in this sense sometimes considered to be an enabling right,[45] its main characteristic is its close association with human dignity and human flourishing on its own terms even apart from these important added dimensions. As legal philosopher Julie Cohen explains (using language not unlike that of John Stuart Mill a century and a half earlier), privacy offers space for individual self-reflection and experimentation, allowing humans to develop individuality and intellectual diversity.[46] Or, as Ben Goold puts it, privacy is central to our ability 'to live rich, fulfilling lives'.[47] More generally it can be understood as a right of respite from external pressures, fostering the development of a strong sense of identity, with benefits not just for individuals and groups but also for a progressive society.[48] American psychologist Abraham Maslow, writing on human capabilities in 1970, indeed noted that privacy is for many people in modern society central to human 'self-actualisation' – characterising this as a human need in the hierarchy of needs.[49] Further, he pointed out, those fortunate enough to achieve self-actualisation, the highest level of the hierarchy of needs (coming after the satisfaction of more basic needs such as safety, belongingness, respect, knowledge, understanding), almost always 'positively like . . . privacy'.[50]

All this implies that the value of privacy transcends the social norms of a given community. Nevertheless, the protection of privacy is strengthened when supported by norms. And it does seem that over the course of its development the idea of a right to privacy has become closely associated with the values of multiple communities. There may still be cultural variations, as noted comparative lawyer James Whitman argues, here comparing cultural ideas of privacy as developed in the US over this period with those found in Europe. The first, he suggests, focussed on privacy of the home against the state, reflecting a particularly American libertarianism, the second concerned business

---

45 See Ben Goold, 'Surveillance and the Political Value of Privacy' (2009) *ALF* 3; Neil Richards, *Intellectual Privacy: Rethinking Civil Liberties in the Digital Age* (New York: OUP 2015) 103–4; Manon Oostveen and Kristina Irion, 'The Golden Age of Personal Data: How to Regulate an Enabling Fundamental Right?' in Mor Bakhoum, Beatriz Conde Gallego, Mark-Oliver Mackenrodt, Gintarė Surblytė-Namavičienė (eds), *Personal Data in Competition, Consumer Protection and Intellectual Property Law: Towards a Holistic Approach?* (Berlin: Springer 2018) 7.

46 Julie E Cohen, *Configuring the Networked Self* (New Haven, Conn: YUP 2012).

47 Goold (n 45) 4.

48 See generally Richardson (n 26) ch 5.

49 Abraham Maslow, *Motivation and Personality* (New York: Harper & Row 1970).

50 ibid 160.

and media practices, and were founded more generally on dignitarian ideas.[51] Even so, there was plenty of cross-cutting, with dignity and liberty a feature of both American and European (as well as English) reasoning – and some basic common understanding of 'privacy' for all the cultural variations, as centred around the benefits for individuals and for groups of being allowed to foster a private life free from public intrusion.[52] By the mid-1970s, social researcher Raymond Williams in *Keywords*, his ground-breaking study of social and cultural meaning, identified 'private' as 'the ultimate generalised privilege, however abstract in practice, of seclusion and protection from others (the public); of lack of accountability to "them"; and of related gains in closeness and comfort of these general kinds'[53] – using language comparable to Canadian sociologist Erving Goffman in 1959 talked of a 'backstage' area of life which could be shared with friends and intimates away from the pressures of 'frontstage' life.[54] This idea of a backstage area of life is still a core meaning associated with 'privacy'/'private life' – characterised in the *Urban Dictionary*, as representing the 'part of someone's life that is none of your f. . . business', encompassing a person's private habits and lifestyles and choices of friendships.[55] Or, as American philosopher Martha Nussbaum puts it neatly (echoing Maslow), 'free human lives need spaces for the protection of intimate association'.[56]

In summary, there is much to suggest that the value of being able to enjoy a private life, free from unwanted intrusion from outside, transcends social norms, operating on a higher moral plane. Those arguing for the right to privacy may not adopt the language of a 'natural right' sometimes employed in contemporary discussions of human rights).[57] They may refer generally to the 1948 Universal Declaration of Human Rights with its 'recognition of the inherent dignity and of

---

51 James Q Whitman, 'The Two Western Cultures of Privacy: Dignity Versus Liberty' (2004) 113 *Yale LJ* 1151.

52 See Richardson (n 26) chs 2–4.

53 Raymond Williams, *Keywords: A Vocabulary of Culture and Society* (London: Fontana 1976).

54 Erving Goffman, *The Presentation of Self in Everyday Life* (New York: Anchor 1959).

55 Urban Dictionary at <https://www.urbandictionary.com> ('private life').

56 Martha Nussbaum, *Creating Capabilities: The Human Development Approach* (Cambridge, Mass: HUP 2011) 148.

57 See Marie-Bénédicte Dembour, 'What Are Human Rights? Four Schools of Thought' (2010) 32 *Hum Rights Ql* 1; Dinah L Shelton, *Advanced Introduction to International Human Rights Law* (Cheltenham, UK, Northampton, Mass: Edward Elgar Publishing 2014) 2–7; Peter Jones, *Rights* (Basingstoke, UK: Macmillan 1994) 72 and generally ch 4.

the equal and inalienable rights of all members of the human family' as the basis of the rights enumerated in the Declaration, including the right to privacy/*la vie privée* in Article 12[58] – reaffirmed in the 1950 European Convention on Human Rights of the Council of Europe, including its Article 8 right to private life/*la vie privée*.[59] But, as in previous times, their essential concern in advocating for the right to privacy is by and large (albeit with variations) a concern about human dignity and liberal flourishing, reflecting an idea of the good life that stretches back over several centuries.[60] As philosopher Beate Roessler summarises the position, 'the right to privacy', understood as a right against 'certain kinds of intrusion', seems to occupy 'an entirely natural place . . . within the structure of human rights', its 'moral' status a matter of 'almost worldwide consensus', adding that indeed it is 'one of the most important rights', which because of its human 'emancipatory dimension' occupies a central place within a system of human rights.[61]

2.3   Expanding meaning

Can the same be said of 'privacy' when employed in a more extended sense, responding to what sociologist Georg Simmel in 1903 referred to as the 'deepest problems of modern life', deriving from efforts of individuals to maintain 'independence and individuality' in the face of 'the sovereign power of society . . . [and the weight of] the external culture and technique of life'?[62] Or should a new vocabulary be developed to encompass these kinds of concerns? In fact, what we see from the late 1960s is a proliferation of posited alternative meanings of privacy, going beyond the core idea of intrusion into private life, some of which have become quite influential, others far more contestable, leaving scope for ongoing debate on the outer parameters of the right.

---

58 Universal Declaration of Human Rights (United Nations General Assembly) 1948, Art 12.
59 European Convention on Human Rights (Council of Europe) 1950, Art 8. See also International Covenant on Civil and Political Rights (United Nations General Assembly) 1966, Art 17.
60 Ariès (n 18).
61 Beate Roessler, 'Privacy as a Human Right' (2017) 117 *Proc Aristot Soc* 187, 193–94.
62 Georg Simmel, 'The Metropolis and Mental Life' (first published 1903) in *On Individuality and Social Forms* (Edward A Shils tr, ed with Donald N Levine, Chicago, Ill: University of Chicago Press 1971) 324.

2.3.1   Control over personal information/data

Probably the most influential extended meaning is that put forward by political scientist and lawyer (and Simmel aficionado) Alan Westin in *Privacy and Freedom*.[63] Writing in 1967, Westin argued that with the rise of surveillance technologies in modern America 'privacy' should be understood to encompass 'the claim of individuals, groups, or institutions to determine for themselves when, how, and to what extent information about them is communicated to others'.[64] Interestingly, Westin started by suggesting that fundamentally privacy was concerned with 'the voluntary and temporary withdrawal of a person from the general society through physical or physiological means',[65] drawing on Goffman's distinction between the frontstage and backstage areas of human life. Yet, as he developed his position, it becomes clear that his understanding of what privacy meant and entailed would be significantly different from Goffman's. Thus, rather than simply arguing that encroachments on private life were created by current electronic surveillance technologies and practices, the position taken for instance by Australian Sir Zelman Cowen in his Boyer Lectures in Sydney in 1969,[66] Westin took a very different line in advocating for protection of personal information across the board – putting forward a meaning of privacy that was both narrower and broader than traditionally conceived: being more specifically focussed on the protection of information and more broadly extending to (all) personal information. And, indeed, one might argue that Westin's characterisation of 'privacy' in this fashion was more pertinent to the specific concern being raised by Cowen as well, *viz* that 'our political masters demand of us an ever-growing accounting of our lives and affairs'.[67]

Westin's reasoning that the language of 'privacy' could be adapted to capture such concerns has enjoyed its greatest influence in the US. For instance, in *Katz v United States*, in 1967,[68] the Fourth Amendment's prohibition on unreasonable searches and seizures was deemed a constitutional 'right to privacy' against state intrusion by search and seizure that extended to the use of an electronic listening device

---

63 Alan F Westin, *Privacy and Freedom* (New York: Atheneum 1967).
64 ibid 7.
65 ibid 32–34.
66 Sir Zelman Cowen, *The Private Man* (Boyer Lectures, Sydney: ABC 1969).
67 ibid 5.
68 *Katz v United States* (n 24).

attached to a phone-box used to monitor a suspected criminal's betting activities, a position accepted as settled law and extended to telephone tower surveillance of a suspected criminal's day to day activities in *Carpenter v United States* in 2018.[69] And by the mid-1970s, in *Whalen v Roe*,[70] the Supreme Court was talking about the 'threat to privacy' implied in 'the accumulation of vast amounts of personal information in computerised data banks'. Likewise, the US Privacy Act 1974,[71] enumerating a set of fair processing principles for the collection, storage, use and transmission of personal information in records by federal government agencies, was characterised as a statute about 'privacy', in a fairly straightforward application of Westin's arguments – as were other statutes concerned with control over personal information, including the Video Privacy Protection Act 1988,[72] Children's Online Privacy Protection Act 1998,[73] and California Consumer Privacy Act 2018.[74] Nor was this just a US perspective. By 1980 the OECD in its *Guidelines Governing the Protection of Privacy and Transborder Data Flows of Personal Data,* prepared by an expert group chaired by Australian Judge Michael Kirby, alternated between language of 'privacy' and 'data protection' in enumerating principles for control over the collection, storage use and transmission of personal information across national borders.[75] The Guidelines (now in updated form) have become a reference point for 'privacy', or 'data privacy', standards in jurisdictions across the world.[76]

In Europe the more accepted language is 'data protection', the language of the General Data Protection Regulation 2016,[77] and previously the Data Protection Directive of 1995,[78] and before that various national data protection statutes beginning with the region of Hesse in Germany followed by federal legislation in Sweden in 1973 and Germany in 1977.[79] The language arguably reflects an idea that there

---

69 *Carpenter v United States* (n 24).

70 *Whalen v Roe*, 429 US 589 (1976).

71 5 *USC* § 552a (Privacy Act 1974).

72 8 USC § 2710 (Video Privacy Protection Act 1988).

73 15 USC 6501–6505 (Children's Online Privacy Protection Act 1998).

74 CA Civ Code § 1798.100ff (California Consumer Privacy Act 2018).

75 Organisation for Economic Cooperation and Development (OECD), *Guidelines Governing the Protection of Privacy and Transborder Data Flows of Personal Data* 1980 (revised 2013).

76 See Lee Bygrave, *Data Privacy Law: An International Perspective* (Oxford, UK: OUP 2014) xxv.

77 *General Data Protection Regulation* (EU) 2016/679.

78 Directive on the Protection of Individuals with Regard to the Processing of Personal Data 95/46/EC.

79 See (for a discussion of the legislation), J Lee Riccardi, 'The German Federal Data Protection Act of 1977: Protecting the Right to Privacy?' (1983) 6 *BC Int'l & Comp L Rev* 243.

are wider concerns about misuse of personal data than captured in the traditional language of 'private life', having to do with abuses of power by state and other authorities – and forming a focus of Franz Kafka's and Max Weber's writings on bureaucracy,[80] and Cornelia Vismann's remarkable history of filing systems.[81] The discourse of 'data protection' as a technique of disciplining and improving data management systems (reflecting a Weberian utopian idea that the systems can indeed be improved) has a more particularised history in the European experiences of totalitarian governments during and after World War II. But now it has taken on a broader meaning and value – whether defined in terms of 'informational self-determination' as stated in the German 'Census Act' of 1983,[82] or 'fair processing, consent, legitimacy and non-discrimination' as helpfully framed by Belgian data protection scholars Paul de Hert and Serge Gutwirth in 2009 (giving a sense that data protection laws are there to discipline a range of technocratic abuses of power in a modern bureaucratic society).[83]

That privacy of private life and data protection are viewed as distinct rights in Europe is suggested also by the EU Charter of Fundamental Rights 2000 which provides for rights to private life and data protection in Articles 7 and 8, respectively.[84] Likewise, the Council of Europe's modernised Convention 108 on Data Protection alludes to a person's 'right to control of his or her personal data'; and 'the fundamental values of respect for privacy and protection of personal data'.[85] As several European scholars have noted, the language of two separate rights seems to point to separate albeit overlapping spheres of operation between independent rights with their own character and rationales, one to do with maintaining a sphere of private life free from intrusion, the other having more to do with informational control and

---

80 See Franz Kafka, *The Trial (Der Process)* (Verlag Die Schmiede, Berlin, 1925); Max Weber, *Economy and Society: An Outline of Interpretive Sociology* (*Wirtschaft und Gesellschaft. Grundriß der verstehenden Soziologie*) (Tübingen, 1922), and generally Malcolm Warner, 'Kafka, Weber and Organization Theory' (2007) 60 Hum Relat 1019.

81 Cornelia Vismann, *Files: Law and Media Technology* (Geoffrey Winthrop-Young tr, Stanford, Cal: SUP 2008).

82 Census Act Case (1983) 65 BVerfGE 1; and see Donald P Kommers and Russell A Miller, *The Constitutional Jurisprudence of the Federal Republic of Germany*, 3rd edn (Durham and London: Duke UP 2012) 408.

83 Paul De Hert and Serge Gutwirth, 'Data Protection in the Case Law of Strasbourg and Luxembourg' in Serge Gutwirth, Yves Poullet, Paul De Hert, Cécile de Terwangne, Sjaak Nouwt (eds), *Reinventing Data Protection?* (Dordrecht: Springer 2009).

84 The Charter of Fundamental Rights of the European Union 2000, Arts 7 and 8.

85 Council of Europe Convention 108, 1980, updated 2018, preamble.

proper information-management processes and practices.[86] Although others have suggested, more in line with the US reasoning, that data protection can be viewed as a subject of a more extended right to privacy (or 'data privacy' as it may be termed), these scholars are still in a minority (or at least less evident) in Europe. For its part, the European Court of Justice has in some early cases considering the Charter rights been less than clear about the relationship between Articles 7 and 8 *inter alia* in cases of data retention, transborder data flows and 'the right to be forgotten'.[87] On the other hand, the Court's referencing to 'a data subject's *rights* to privacy and the protection of personal data' (emphasis added) in the recent 'worldwide right to be forgotten' case of *CNIL v Google*,[88] suggests that it acknowledges that there are indeed two distinct albeit potentially overlapping rights here.

As to the European Court of Human Rights, it has tended to treat the (single) right to private life under Article 8 of the European Convention on Human Rights in very broad terms, covering a range of social and professional interactions,[89] as well as rights to image and reputation (or at least where there is sufficiently connected to private life that the right to private life can be said to be engaged).[90] Per the Grand Chamber in *Von Hannover v Germany (No 2)* in 2012, 'the guarantee afforded by Article 8 of the Convention is primarily intended to ensure the development, without outside interference, of the personality of each individual in his relations with other human beings'.[91] Thus, developing a line of reasoning from earlier cases such

---

86 See De Hert and Gutwirth (n 83); Mireille Hildebrandt and Bert-Jaap Koops, 'The Challenges of Ambient Law and Legal Protection in the Profiling Era' (2010) 73 *MLR* 428, 439; Orla Lynskey, 'Deconstructing Data Protection: the "Added-Value" of a Right to Data Protection in the EU Legal Order' (2014) 63 *ICLQ* 569.

87 See, for instance, Case C-293/12 *Digital Rights Ireland*, 8 April 2014; Case C-131/12 *Google Spain SL, Google Inc v Agencia Española de Protección de Datos (AEPD) and Mario Costeja González*, 13 May 2014; Case C-1/15 Opinion pursuant to Art 218(11) TFEU, 26 July 2017; Case C-498/16 *Schrems v Facebook Ireland Limited*, 25 January 2018; Case C-345/17 *Buivids v Datu valsts inspekcija*, 14 February 2019; Case C-673/17 *Planet49 GmbH*, 1 October 2019.

88 Case C-507/17 *CNIL v Google LLC*, 24 September 2019 [67], [69] (Grand Chamber); see also Case C-136/17 *CJ and Others v CNIL*, 24 September 2019 [37], [44]–[46], [59], [67]–[69] (Grand Chamber).

89 *Niemietz v Germany* (1993) 16 EHRR 97; *Copland v UK* [2007] ECHR 253; *Peck v United Kingdom* (2003) 36 EHRR 41; *Copland v UK* [2007] ECHR 253; *Bărbulescu v Romania* [2017] *ECHR* 754.

90 *Von Hannover v Germany* (2004) 40 EHRR 1; *Von Hannover v Germany (No 2)* (2012) 55 EHRR 15; *Axel Springer v Germany* (2012) 55 EHRR 183.

91 *Von Hannover v Germany (No 2)* (n 90) [95].

as *Niemietz v Germany* in 1993,[92] and *Von Hannover v Germany* in 2004,[93] the Court states that 'there is . . . a zone of interaction of a person with others, even in a public context, which may fall within the scope of private life'.[94] Should this be taken as suggesting that the right to private life under Article 8 encompasses *inter alia* a right to data protection? Or is it that the European Court of Human Rights is simply acknowledging that the dividing line between 'private life' and 'public life' may sometimes be blurred – for instance, where activities involve a public figure who nevertheless seeks to claim a sphere of private life including in quite public settings (as in the first *Von Hannover* case, where Princess Caroline objected to constant media surveillance and reporting of details of her daily life), or involve social relationships of various kinds (as in the *Von Hannover* cases), or are of a professional not merely a personal character (as in *Niemietz*, involving a police search of a lawyer's home and business premises) – and is positing that in these cases the treatment of the Article 8 right will necessarily have to deal with both dimensions?

2.3.2   Physical, sensory privacy

Surveillance warrants special attention in discussions of privacy (and data protection). As Bentham remarked in his 18th century study of the Panopticon prison,[95] the sense an individual may have of being being constantly watched by another agent places the subject essentially under the controlling eye of the watcher – his work, along with Orwell's *Nineteen Eighty-Four*,[96] becoming a reference point for later studies of totalitarian surveillance and policing.[97] While often surveillance studies scholars eshew the language of 'privacy' in favour of a close examination of the relations of power and control in their discussions of surveillance, David Lyon is among those who have come to regard it (for all its limitations) as still helpful in talking about the deprivations a subject may suffer.[98] Likewise, privacy scholars focusing on

---

92 *Niemietz v Germany* (n 89) [29].

93 *Von Hannover v Germany* (n 90) [50].

94 *Von Hannover v Germany (No 2)* (n 90) [95].

95 Jeremy Bentham, *Panopticon; or, The Inspection House* (first published 1791) in John Bowring (ed), *Works of Jeremy Bentham* (Edinburgh: William Tait 1843) vol 4, 40.

96 George Orwell, *Nineteen Eighty-Four* (London: Secker & Warburg 1949).

97 See, for instance, Michel Foucault, *Discipline and Punish: The Birth of the Prison* (Alan Sheridan tr, New York: Vintage 1979); David Lyon, *The Electronic Eye: The Rise of Surveillance Society* (Cambridge, UK: Polity 1984).

98 See David Lyon, *The Culture of Surveillance: Watching as a Way of Life* (Cambridge, UK: Polity 2018).

surveillance practices quite often characterise concerns about surveillance as (in part at least) about privacy, commenting on the dangers of widely-distributed 'uninterrupted monitoring' undermining the subject's ability to make informed choices and inhibiting . . . autonomy,[99] restricting our abilities 'to live rich, fulfilling lives',[100] and to function as citizens of civil society, and advocating stronger legal protection.[101] Moreover, as Ben Goold points out, surveillance need not be understood here in the totalitarian sense evoked by scholars of the 1970s, or by Orwell in his dystopian masterwork: 'Although surveillance has become ubiquitous, it has also become increasingly decentralised and ambiguous. In a world of online shopping, social networking websites, and GPS enabled smart phones, it is hard to point to a single Big Brother who fully embodies our fears about the loss of privacy and can serve as a focus for acts of resistance'.[102] Yet surveillance of these kinds can still have a potential chilling effect on political discourse, and 'on the ability of groups to express their views through protest and other forms of peaceful civil action'.[103]

Some scholars have gone further in adopting the language of 'physical' or 'sensory' privacy to convey a sense of a person's integrity being violated by the encroachments of others.[104] As noted earlier, physical privacy has an ancient lineage, associated with 'walling off' private spaces such as the home where private life is traditionally conducted. The interior aspects of the physical body and mind can also be associated with physical privacy. Indeed, in recent times, some have noted a sense of physical, or sensory, personal boundaries being breached even in physically public and social environments – for instance, Lord Hope's comment in *Campbell v MGN Ltd* that there is an effect on a person's 'sensibilities', especially a drug addict (like Naomi Campbell in that case) trying to recover, where she becomes aware that 'somebody, somewhere, was following her, was well aware of what was going on

---

99   Claire EM Jervis, '*Barbalescu v Romainia*: 'Why There is no Room for Complacency When it Comes to Privacy Rights in the Workplace' (2018) 47 *Industrial Law Journal* 440, 449-50.

100   Goold (n 45) 4.

101   ibid. cf Neil Richards, 'The Dangers of Surveillance' (2013) 126 *Harv L Rev* 1934; Andrew Roberts, 'A Republican Account of the Value of Privacy' (2015) 14 *Eur J Pol Theor* 320.

102   Goold (n 45) 4.

103   ibid. See also UN Human Rights Committee (HRC), CCPR General Comment No. 16: Article 17 (Right to Privacy).

104   See, for instance, Nicole Moreham, 'The Nature of the Privacy Interest' in NA Moreham and Sir Mark Warby (eds), *The Law of Privacy and the Media*, 3rd edn (Oxford, UK: OUP 2016) ch 2 at 42-57 and *passim.*

and was prepared to disclose the facts to the media'?[105] Likewise, in *Von Hannover v Germany* the European Court of Human Rights noted Princess Caroline's arguments that the media's persistent monitoring of her private life occurred over an extended period and involved multiple actors – Princess Caroline complaining that 'as soon as she left her house she was constantly hounded by paparazzi who followed her every daily movement, be it crossing the road, fetching her children from school, doing her shopping, out walking, engaging in sport or going on holiday'.[106] And, as James Boyle says, if the practices involve also relentless categorisation and judgement (whether by the media, or the state, or other powerful entities, groups or individuals), there may be a heightened sense of always being under the eye of others who are not only capable of but actually exercise real control.[107]

As to intellectual and decisional privacy,[108] these are more contestable concepts. Is not all privacy geared to fostering intellectual and decisional freedom on a liberal conception?[109] Arguably some support may be found in US Supreme Court cases of *Griswold v Connecticut*[110] and *Roe v Wade*,[111] where it was held that the choices that people might want to make about contraception and abortion were a matter of privacy protected under the Constitution.[112] On the other hand, there is a bodily or sensory dimension to these cases as well, focused on sexuality and reproduction, as well as an informational dimension, having to do with how information is processed in intellectual reflection and decision-making about these most intimate aspects of private life.[113] Indeed, in *Roe*, the Court stated that its concern was with a woman's right to 'right to do with one's body as one pleases', bearing 'a close relationship to the right of privacy previously articulated in the

---

105 *Campbell v MGN Ltd* [2004] 2 AC 457, [98] (Lord Hope).

106 *Von Hannover v Germany* (n 90), [44].

107 See James Boyle, 'Foucault in Cyberspace: Surveillance, Sovereignty, and Hardwired Censors' (1997) 66 *U Cinn L Rev* 177.

108 Anita Allen, 'Taking Liberties: Privacy, Private Choice, and Social Contract Theory' (1987) 56 *U Cin L Rev* 561; Beate Rössler, *The Value of Privacy* (Rupert Glasgow tr, Oxford: Polity 2005); and further Roessler (n 61); Richards (n 45) and further Richards (n 101); Bart van der Sloot, 'Decisional Privacy 2.0: The Procedural Requirements Implicit in Article 8 ECHR and its Potential Impact on Profiling' (2017) 7 *IDPL* 190.

109 See Raymond Wacks, 'The Poverty of Privacy' (1980) 96 *LQR* 73; W A Parent, 'Privacy, Morality, and the Law' (1983) 12 *Phil & Pub Aff* 269.

110 *Griswold v Connecticut*, 81 US 479 (1965).

111 *Roe v Wade* 410 US 113 (1973).

112 See especially Allen (n 108).

113 And see Neil Richards, 'The Information Privacy Law Project' (2006) 94 *Geo LJ* 1087, 1107–15.

Court's decisions'.[114] Likewise, in the 2003 case of *Lawrence v Texas*,[115] where Texan and other state sodomy laws extending within the home were held to be unconstitutional under the due process clause of the 14th Amendment, the language of privacy in the home and of 'intimate conduct with another person' features in the Supreme Court's discussion of the nature of the privacy at issue in this case. (Compare also cases involving Article 8 of the European Convention on Human Rights involving matters such forced sterilisation of ethnic minority women and pollution in the home affecting enjoyment of private and family life, which have also been characterised by some scholars as cases of 'decisional privacy'.)[116]

2.3.3   Towards 'privacy' pluralism?

In *Privacy and Context*, Helen Nisenbaum observes that social understandings of 'privacy' are shaped by and respond to technologies and practices that 'diminish control' and 'threaten disruption to the very fabric of social life', producing 'context-relative . . . norms' of privacy.[117] As such, she echoes Saussure's point that the 'meaning' of a sign is its meaning as understood by the 'community of speakers',[118] in the process becoming (as Roland Barthes adds) 'constitutive' of reason in its own right.[119] Nissenbaum is talking here about information technologies and practices generating informational norms of privacy, but the same point can be made about technologies and practices shaping privacy norms more generally. Likewise, Daniel Solove in *Understanding Privacy* posits that privacy is best appreciated in a 'pluralistic and contextual manner' grounded in 'socially recognized different kinds of privacy violations'.[120] Solove's privacy categories are fairly conventional (at least in the US), identifying control over personal information with regard to 'information collection', 'information processing', 'information dissemination', along with 'physical intrusion' and 'decisional interference' as current

---

114   *Roe v Wade* (n 111), the Court at 154.

115   *Lawrence v Texas*, 539 US 558 (2003).

116   For instance, *Guerra v Italy* (1998) 26 *EHRR* 357; *Gomez v Spain* (2005) 41 EHRR 40; *VC v Slovakia* (2014) 59 *EHRR* 29; and van der Sloot (n 108).

117   Helen Nissenbaum, *Privacy in Context: Technology, Policy and the Integrity of Social Life* (Berkeley, Cal: University of California Press 2010) 3.

118   Saussure (n 4) 67, 71.

119   Roland Barthes, *The Fashion System* (first published Paris: Seuil 1967, Matthew Ward and Richard Howard tr, New York: Hill and Wang 1983) xi.

120   Daniel K Solove, *Understanding Privacy* (Cambridge, Mass: HUP 2008) 10.

types of privacy.[121] But his reasoning suggests a possibility of pro-liferating pluralist meanings that might go well beyond the actually rather restricted meanings he sees as being associated with privacy to date.[122] Nevertheless, his point that the social meaning of privacy may well continue to change is an important one – even if some of us might want to argue that it would be better to adopt a new vocabu-lary, more attuned to the issues of identity preservation and forma-tion in the face of new threats from current and future technologies and practices. The task of mapping change is one I will come back to later in this book, considering the ways in which language and mean-ing might evolve further in the digital age as we embark on a period of increased automation.

For now, I limit my observations to the current position, focussing on where we have got to with the meaning and value of privacy to date. Here a useful starting point is the synthesis offered by Roessler. In short, Roessler suggests that 'privacy' currently, as in the past, may still be best understood as freedom from intrusion. Nevertheless, she singles out 'certain kinds of intrusion', which she classifies as intru-sion into 'physical space', that is, 'local or domestic privacy', intrusion into informational privacy 'limiting the amount of information about a person that others – be they persons or institutions – have or are able to obtain', and intrusion into 'decisional privacy' concerning 'private decisions and actions'.[123] Certainly, Roessler's language of 'intrusion' suggests that the traditional meaning of privacy as freedom from intru-sion into private life has a special place in her typology, offering a kind of central ordering-principle that sits above and continues to shape the more particular types of privacy (which operate in effect as mid-level principles underneath the meta-principle).[124] However, she accepts Nissembaum's argument that '[a]ny normative conception of privacy needs to be able to accommodate new developments and contexts regarding social norms of privacy . . . [and] new interpretations of what privacy means'[125] – although (as a philosopher and an historian) she still wants to maintain that there is an enduring idea of privacy as con-cerned essentially with intrusion which has grown up over the course

---

121 ibid.
122 See, for instance, Bert-Jaap Koops, Bryce Clayton Newell, Tjerk Timan, Ivan Skorvánek, Tomislav Chokrevski, and Maša Galič, 'A Typology of Privacy' (2017) 38 *UPJIL* 483.
123 Roessler (n 61) 190–92.
124 See Michael Bayles, 'Mid-level Principles and Justification' (1986) 28 *NOMOS* 49.
125 Roessler (n 61) 190.

of history, its strength as a principle attributable to its 'emancipatory dimension'.

I find Roessler's approach very appealing in its focus on social meaning as constrained (to an extent) by tradition, and acceptance that the traditional meaning of privacy as freedom from intrusion into private life still has an important and central place in today's world, consistent with modern liberal and dignitarian values. I might want to interrogate some aspects of her typology – in particular asking whether 'decisional privacy' needs to be identified as a separate type of privacy, suggesting that 'sensory privacy' should be recognised alongside 'physical privacy', and wondering whether when we talk about 'informational privacy' and 'physical/sensory privacy' we may be inclined to consider these in some broader sense going to identity formation and preservation. That said, Roessler captures crucially the idea of the right to privacy as at heart concerned with freedom from intrusion into private life, while at the same time having much to say about physical/sensory integrity and informational control, underpinned by human dignity and liberty. Likewise, if I were to put forward my own attempt at synthesis of every-thing discussed in this chapter, it would be that the right to privacy is evolving but it is still at core concerned with freedom from intrusion into private life despite its more contested penumbra.

3   Regulating for privacy

When Beate Roessler asks, 'what does it mean to be free from intrusion?',[1] she asks a question that can be answered in very different ways. As a philosopher, Roessler is primarily concerned with exploring the moral dimension of the right to privacy. On the other hand, an engineer or designer might be more inclined to look to the design of technical systems around privacy – as when William Mitchell says '[s]ometimes we want to be private; sometimes we want to put ourselves on display', adding 'what's required are sophisticated systems that are able to control the level of public visibility' we have 'at any moment'.[2] For a sociologist, the answer might come down to observing social norms. Thus Erving Goffman talks of shared social understandings about the difference between the 'front stage' and 'back stage' areas of life which should not generally be breached.[3] And Helen Nissenbaum talks of context-specific norms of privacy more generally.[4] A psychologist, such as Irving Altman, might stress a person's psychological aversion to breaching mental boundaries that individuals and groups may choose to erect around the spheres of their lives they consider to be private while including other within – another version of an argument about social behaviour and norms.[5] A political scientist or surveillance studies scholar might focus on reining in power as derived from multiple sources including law and increasingly technologies, as in the work of David Lyon.[6] An economist talking about privacy will most likely be thinking in terms of efficient markets – for instance, Guy Rolnick and Luigi Zingales of

---

1 Beate Roessler, 'Privacy as a Human Right' (2017) 117 *Proc Aristot Soc* 187, 190.

2 Victor Chase, "Why Buck Rogers Will Be Invisible: Interview with William J Mitchell', *Pictures of the Future* (Spring 2004) 34 <https://www.docme.ru/doc/86920>.

3 Erving Goffman, *The Presentation of Self in Everyday Life* (New York: Anchor 1959).

4 Helen Nissenbaum, *Privacy in Context: Technology, Policy and the Integrity of Social Life* (Stanford, Calif: SUP 2010).

5 Irving Altman, *The Environment and Social Behavior: Privacy, Personal Space, Territory, Crowding* (Monterey, Calif: Brooks/Cole 1975).

6 David Lyon, *The Culture of Surveillance: Watching as a Way of Life* (Cambridge, UK: Polity 2018).

the University of Chicago arguing in the *New York Times* that that people should 'own' their data.[7]

But this chapter is concerned primarily with law. And, of course, for a lawyer, a typical response to the question of how to be free from intrusion is to think in terms of legal regulation. And for lawyers who look across different fields, for instance lawyer economists well-versed in law and markets,[8] or legal philosophers considering the ideal relationship between moral rights and legal rights,[9] or legal sociologists considering the extent to which law reflects social norms,[10] or lawyers who pay particular attention to psychology,[11] or lawyers who work is focussed on surveillance, seeking to navigate between surveillance as a tool of real power and purported regulation of law,[12] and increasingly nowadays technology lawyers looking to technology as well as law,[13] the answer is to emphasise how legal regulation can be combined with other techniques in an effort to determine what law (or laws) will work best in regulating for privacy. That is the approach adopted in this chapter, although the principal focus is squarely on the law's operation.

3.1   Modalities of regulation

Such reasoning allows for quite sophisticated regulatory approaches. For instance, in *Code and Other Laws of Cyberspace*, first published in 1999,[14] and updated in a version 'written in part through a collaborative Wiki' as *Codev2* in 2006,[15] cyber-lawyer Lawrence Lessig maps

7   Luigi Zingales and Guy Rolnik, 'A Way to Own Your Social-Media Data' *New York Times* (New York, 30 June 2017). See also Eric A Posner and E Glen Weyl, *Radical Markets: Uprooting Capitalism and Democracy for a Just Society* (Princeton NJ: Princeton University Press 2018) ch 5.

8   For instance, Richard A Posner, 'The Economics of Privacy' (1981) 17 *Am Econ Rev* 405l; Alessandro Acquisti, Curtis Taylor and Liad Wagman, 'The Economics of Privacy' (2016) 54 *JEL* 442.

9   For instance, Ruth Gavison, 'Privacy and the Limits of Law' (1980) 89 *Yale LJ* 421; Lisa Austin, 'Privacy and the Question of Technology' (2003) 22 *Law & Phil* 119.

10   For instance, Daniel K Solove, *Understanding Privacy* (Cambridge, Mass: HUP 2008).

11   For instance, Kirsty Hughes, 'A Behavioural Understanding of Privacy and its Implications for Privacy Law' (2012) 75 *MLR* 806.

12   For instance, Ben Goold 'Surveillance and the Political Value of Privacy' (2009) *ALF* 3.

13   For instance, Woodrow Hartzog, *Privacy's Blueprint: The Battle to Control the Design of New Technologies* (Cambridge, Mass: HUP 2018).

14   Lawrence Lessig, *Code and Other Laws of Cyberspace* (New York: Basic Books 1999) ch 7.

15   Lawrence Lessig, *Codev2* (New York: Basic Books, 2006) <http://codev2.cc> ch 7.

four 'modalities' of regulation – 'the law, social norms, the market and architecture' (ie, the built environment, or technology), arguing that regulation is 'the sum of these four constraints'.[16] He points out that sometimes the modalities may operate in conflict with each other. But they can also work in tandem in constraining or enabling freedom. Further, he adds, some might work better than others – for instance, in some contexts, social norms, in others law, and in others still technology, as increasingly seems to be the case in digital environment. Lessig is not talking especially about the regulation of privacy here (although he does come back to privacy later as we shall see). But his elegant model can be used to analyse how privacy laws regulate privacy subjects alongside social, technological and business/markets modalities.

We can use Lessig's analysis to imagine the effect of regulatory modalities on privacy subjects who may be constrained or enabled in their pursuit of privacy by the combination of technology, markets, social norms and law. This may occur in a range of ways, bearing in mind that, as Lessig says, the modalities do not only govern directly but also indirectly. For instance, privacy laws may be geared to influencing not just behaviour but social norms, technologies and/or market practices (and conversely the laws will also be subjected to influences from these other modalities). Moreover, the process of adjustment and readjustment will likely be an ongoing one. Or as Lessig puts it in *Codev2*, quoting Polk Wagner,[17] 'the interaction among these modalities is dynamic, "requiring consideration of not only . . . legal adjustments, but also predicting the responsive effects these changes will stimulate"', with the legal regulator seeking an 'equilibrium' among the modalities.[18] Thus we can posit a dynamic feedback loop in which technological changes are followed by adjustments in markets, social norms and legal standards – examples of what French sociologist Michel Callon and his co-authors describe as 'iterations, movements to and fro, negotiations and compromises of all sorts'.[19] The language suggests that changes will typically be more in the way of 'iterations' than grand steps, that is, involving small incremental adjustments (although these

---

16 Ibid, 123.

17 Polk Wagner, 'On Software Regulation' (2005) 78 *SCL Rev* 457, 465.

18 See Lessig, *Codev2* (n 15) 130.

19 M Callon, P Laredo, V Rabeharisoa, T Gonard and T Leray, 'The Management and Evaluation of Technological Programs and the Dynamics of Techno-Economic Networks: The Case of AFME' (1992) 21 *Res Pol* 215.

can have quite significant effects) – and that here law is no different from other modalities.[20] Even so, the experience of history shows that legal reinvention does happen from time to time, and further that the prospect of legal influence cannot be discounted.

3.2   Difference made by rights

Does it change the equation that privacy is talked of as a right? Or, to revert to Lessig, does that change the force of a modality of regulation? In part, it depends on what kind of right we are talking about. For instance, a 'natural right' (if the language is still considered appropriate) carries little formal legal weight in a world in which 'law' is understood as positive law backed by legal sanction. And this seems to be Lessig's world, with law in a positive sense distinguished from other modalities of regulation. The same goes for a 'moral right', or 'human right', to privacy, that is, a right deriving authority from values such as human dignity and liberty (which is probably closer to how many modern privacy scholars view the right to privacy). Such extra-legal rights may have a certain influence on social norms and in that way may regulate, either directly or indirectly via the influence of social norms, on law. But a correlation between social norms and law cannot be assumed – and nor can it be assumed either that extra-legal rights will find a corollary in either norms or law. A further step of translation is needed before they can take on the force of legal regulation. As Oliver Wendell Holmes put it in 1897, there is a basic difference between 'the rights of man in a moral sense' and rights and wrongs as prescribed by law.[21]

Moreover, not all legal rights are equally powerful in regulatory terms. For instance, recognition of a human right to privacy at international law founded on human dignity and flourishing, as provided in Article 12 of the Universal Declaration of Human Rights of 1948,[22] or Article 17 of the International Covenant on Civil and Political Rights in 1966,[23] may not significantly change behaviour of states, business and human actors on the ground unless and until the right is made part of domestic

20 See Megan Richardson, 'Responsive Law Reform: A Case Study in Privacy and the Media' (2013) 15 *EJLR* 20.

21 Oliver Wendell Holmes, Jr, 'The Path of the Law' (1897) 10 *Harv L Rev* 457, 460–61.

22 Universal Declaration of Human Rights (UNGA 1948), Art 12.

23 International Covenant on Civil and Political Rights (UNGA 1966), Art 17.

law of a given national jurisdiction.[24] Thus in the UK it was only after the right to private life in Article 8 of the European Convention on Human Rights 1950[25] was formally incorporated into UK law through the Human Rights Act 1998,[26] tasking lawmakers specifically with the legal obligation to reshape their law to comply with its standards, that courts took the final step of developing a tort of misuse of private information to give effect to the Article 8 right rather than relying on the traditional doctrine of breach of confidence from older cases.

Likewise, as to the 'common law' right to privacy (the right that Samuel Warren and Louis Brandeis were talking about in their article on 'The Right to Privacy' in the 1890 *Harvard Law Review*, citing *inter alia* the breach of confidence case of *Prince Albert v Strange* from 1849, which itself used the language of a 'right'),[27] or a constitutional or statutory right to privacy (whether derived from judges, as for instance with the right to privacy found by judges in the general terms of the US Constitution,[28] or as spelt out explicitly, as for instance, in the UK Human Rights Act and various US State Constitutions),[29] their authoritative legal status derives from their acknowledgment of the right to privacy by judges, legislators and constitution-drafters, not from some anterior moral law. We can compare here the civil right to *la vie privée* spelt out in Article 9 of the French *Code civil* in 1970,[30] and before that identified by judges in cases dating back to the 19th century. Judges may have used dignitarian language but traced the legal authority for their decisions to the open language of the Code which they interpreted creatively, in effect, to fashion a legal right to privacy – thus, as former senior member of the *Conseil d'État* Roger Errera puts it, as in the UK, the right to privacy in France was an 'illustration of judicial law-making, applied to an important social and legal issue', with judges responding to a felt need to provide plaintiffs

---

24 See Michael Kirby, 'Constitutional Law and International Law: National Exceptionalism and the Democratic Deficit' (2010) 12 *U Notre Dame Aust L Rev 95, 106–07*.

25 Convention for the Protection of Human Rights and Fundamental Freedoms (CoE 1950).

26 Human Rights Act 1998 c 42, in force October 2000.

27 Samuel D Warren and Louis D Brandeis, 'The Right to Privacy' (1890) 4 *Harv L Rev* 193 (citing *Prince Albert v Strange* (1849) 2 De G & Sm 652; 1 H & Tw 1).

28 See *Boyd v United States*, 116 US 616 (1886); *Olmstead v United States*, 277 US 438 (1928), Brandeis J dissenting; *Katz v United States* 389 US 347 (1967); *Carpenter v United States*, 585 US– (2018); 138 S Ct 2206.

29 See 'Privacy Protections in State Constitutions' (NCSL, 1 July 2018) <https://www.ncsl.org/research/telecommunications-and-information-technology/privacy-protections-in-state-constitutions.aspx>.

30 *Art 9* du *code civil* (loi du 17 juillet 1970).

with remedies for breaches of their privacy in the face of the silence of Parliament.[31]

As the above discussion hints at, legal rights themselves may in fact take a variety of legal forms and may have a variety of legal consequences. First, as we have seen, a legal right to privacy may take the form of a legally recognised human right at international law, a constitutional right, a statutory or common law right embedded in the common law tradition (or a civil law right embedded in a civil law jurisdiction). Second, the legal consequences of legal 'rights' may range from correlative duties on other parties to privileges, powers and/or immunities for the right-holder, the various incidents of a legal right observed by American legal realist Wesley Newcomb Hohfeld in 1913 (drawing on Holmes's analysis of rights and correlative duties).[32] Although Hohfeld identified rights in the strict sense with a right to claim for breach imposing legal duties on others, he acknowledged that 'the term "right" tends to be used indiscriminately to cover what in a given case may be a privilege, a power, or an immunity, rather than a right in the strictest sense'.[33] Indeed, as Leif Wenar says, '[m]ost rights are complex molecular rights . . . made up of multiple Hohfeldian incidents'.[34] To take the example of a common law right to privacy, this may include a claim right, for breach of a correlative obligation imposed on another party, via a tort or equitable wrong, a privilege or immunity from any claim right (or privilege) of another party, and a power to enforce, waive or annul that other party's liability for breach of the claim right. Likewise, a constitutional right to privacy, as represented for instance in Article 8 of the European Convention on Human Rights, or Article 7 of the EU Charter of Fundamental Rights (generally deployed in combination with the Charter Article 8 right to data protection),[35] or found in various Amendments of the US Constitution (albeit not spelt out in the language of privacy),[36] may

---

31 See Roger Errera, 'On the Origins and Contents of Article 9 of the Civil Code on the Right to Privacy' (Franco-Brit L Soc, London, 23 September 2011) <http://www.rogererrera.fr/liberte_expression/docs/Article_9.pdf>.

32 Wesley Newcomb Hohfeld, 'Some Fundamental Legal Conceptions as Applied in Judicial Reasoning' (1913) 23 *Yale LJ* 16; and 'Fundamental Legal Conceptions as Applied in Judicial Reasoning' (1917) *Yale LJ* 26; Oliver Wendell Holmes, 'Codes, and the Arrangement of the Law' (1870) 5 *Am L Rev* 1.

33 Hohfeld, 'Some Fundamental Legal Conceptions' (n 32), 30.

34 Leif Wenar, 'The Nature of Rights' (2005) 33 *Phil & Pub Aff* 223, 234.

35 Charter of Fundamental Rights of the European Union (2000), Arts 7 and 8.

36 US Constitution, especially Fourth Amendment (search and seizure) and 14th Amendment (equality, due process).

include a claim right directed at the state to challenge the exercise of purported state authority, a privilege or immunity from any countervailing right/privilege, and arguably also a (rather limited) power to waive/annul what would otherwise be a breach of the claim right.[37]

'Right' to privacy:	(claim) right	privilege	power	immunity
Correlative:	duty	no right	liability	disability

Figure 3.1   The right to privacy as a Hohfeldian legal right

Third, those who take rights seriously might argue that moral or human rights count for more as legal rights, once they take on a legal form.[38] But even then they will not automatically trump the legal rights, privileges/freedoms of others (which may also reference moral or human rights), or broader public interests. A 'balance' may be required[39] – or to adopt the more structured European language of 'proportionality', an assessment may need to be made of whether an action or measure is in pursuit of a legitimate end, is necessary and proportionate.[40] Moreover, while a moral or human right to privacy may represent 'the ultimate generalised privilege', as Raymond Williams put it in the mid-1970s,[41] this is not necessarily so for a legal right to privacy which may end up being weakened or qualified in significant respects in the process of translation into a legal right (ie depending on the language used). Nevertheless, we can accept that a moral or human right should ideally add something to the importance and weight of a legal right, when it comes to assessments of the value of the right to privacy and its weight in the balance with other rights, freedoms and interests which are also legally recognised and protected.

3.3   Comparing laws

A further point to make is that a legal right to privacy may entail not just one but a range of correlative duties/obligations to respect privacy. In fact, it is quite common to see privacy laws (whether taking the

---

37 See *Jørgen* Aall, 'Waiver of Human Rights' (2011) 29 *Nordic J Hum Rts* 56.

38 See generally Peter Jones, *Rights* (Basingstoke, UK: 1994), 8 and *passim*.

39 See Stijn Smet and Eva Brems (eds), *When Human Rights Clash at the European Court of Human Rights: Conflict or Harmony?* (Oxford, UK: OUP 2017).

40 See Moyshe Cohen-Eliya and Iddo-Porat, 'American Balancing and German Proportionality: The Historical Origins' (2010) 8 *Int'l J Const L* 263.

41 Raymond Williams, *Keywords: A Vocabulary of Culture and Society* (London: Fontana 1976).

form of constitutional, legislative or judge-made law) focussed on specific obligations rather than on the right to privacy expressed in more
general terms. These laws may correspond quite closely to the most
common 'types' of 'privacy' discussed in the previous chapter – *viz*,
'informational privacy' and 'physical/sensory privacy' (both of which if
construed expansively go well beyond the traditional idea of the right
to privacy as a right to private life, although protecting private life may
still be a particular concern). We see this is in the discussion below
as we look at the way that privacy laws have developed in a range of
jurisdictions. In substantive albeit not formal terms the protection is
often quite comparable. On the other hand, there are still differences,
especially in the balance with other rights, freedoms and interests.

3.3.1   The US and its followers

As detailed by William Prosser in 1960,[42] a substantial body of tort
law developed in the various states of the US in the years following
Warren and Brandeis's article – responding to what they described
in rather Lessigian terms as the impetus of 'recent inventions and
business methods' feeding public desires for 'gossip'.[43] Warren and
Brandeis's proposed tort regarding unwanted publications in the press
gave rise to what Prosser called the 'public disclosure of . . . private
facts' tort.[44] Moreover, just a few years after their article, photogravure
and lithographic technologies had developed to the point that personal likenesses were a common feature of advertising in newspapers,
magazines and posters, which prompted another tort, identified by
Prosser as 'appropriation' of 'attributes of the plaintiff's identity'.[45] An
example is the New York Civil Rights Law's 'right to privacy', passed
in 1903, proscribing the use of a person's 'name, portrait or picture
. . . for advertising purposes or for the purposes of trade without the
written consent first obtained',[46] after Abigail Roberson failed before
the court in objecting to the use of her image in Franklin Mills flour
advertisements in *Roberson v Rochester Folding Box Co* in 1902.[47]
But in Georgia, for instance, the same result was achieved through
common law development.[48] There were also two further torts noted

---

42 William Prosser, 'Privacy' (1960) 48 Calif L Rev 383.

43 Warren and Brandeis (n 27) 195.

44 Prosser (n 42) 392.

45 ibid 401.

46 NY Civil Rights Law 1903, § 50 (right to privacy) and § 51 (action for injunction and for damages).

47 *Roberson v Rochester Folding Box Co*, 171 NY 538, 64 NE 442 (1902).

48 *Pavesich v New England Life Insurance Co*, 122 Ga 190 (1905).

by Prosser, one a 'false light' privacy tort in some states, an adaptation of defamation law's protection of reputation but focussed more on the private emotions of the plaintiff,[49] the other – in fact the first in the list – concerning what Prosser termed 'intrusion . . . upon seclusion or solitude'.[50] By 1977, in the Second Restatement on Torts (where Prosser served as Chief Reporter),[51] the same four privacy torts featured, and these torts, continue to frame the protection of privacy (as a matter of private law) in the US.[52]

Nevertheless, reading Prosser's cases there seems to be less uniformity across US states than the taxonomy might suggest. Contrast, for instance, the California case of *Melvin v Reid*, in 1931,[53] where Gabrielle Darley Melvin successfully relied on the tort of public disclosure of private facts after a biopic film revealed details of her previous life as a prostitute involved in a murder trial, with the New York case of *Sidis v FR Publishing Corp*, in 1940,[54] where former child prodigy William Sidis failed in his claim over the *New Yorker*'s exposé of his adult life. It was only after *Sidis* was taken as the model for the US Supreme Court's broadly construed 'newsworthiness' privilege under the First Amendment in *Time, Inc v Hill*, in 1967,[55] that a more uniform deference was accorded to 'newsworthy' free speech in publication of private facts and false light cases across the US. To give another example, in many states, the appropriation of name or likeness tort is largely superseded by a right of publicity covering the same indicia, following the Second Circuit judgment in *Haelan Labs, Inc v Topps Chewing Gum, Inc*,[56] in 1953, where Judge Frank suggested the real harm suffered for 'many prominent persons' was loss of commercial or professional benefits. In California, indeed, there are statutory and common law rights of publicity.[57] But New York remains an outlier with its limited statutory privacy appropriation tort.[58] (Although aspects of Prosser's

---

49 Prosser (n 42) 398.

50 ibid 389.

51 Restatement of the Law, 2nd, Torts (ALI 1977) § 652ff.

52 And see Prosser's '"Privacy" at 50: A Symposium on Privacy in the 21st Century' (2010) 98 *Calif L Rev* 1711ff.

53 *Melvin v Reid*, 112 Cal App 285 (1931).

54 *Sidis v FR Publishing Corp*, 113 F2d 806 (1940).

55 *Time, Inc v Hill* 385 US 374 (1967).

56 See *Haelan Labs, Inc v Topps Chewing Gum, Inc*, 202 F 2d 866 (1953), and generally J Thomas McCarthy, *The Rights of Publicity and Privacy*, 2nd edn (St Paul, Minn: Thomson West 2008).

57 CA Civ Code, § 3344; *Midler v Ford Motor Co*, 849 F 2d 460 (1988); *Waits v Frito-Lay, Inc*, 978 F 2d 1093 (1992).

58 See McCarthy (n 56) vol 1, §6:81.

privacy torts may be dealt with under other laws, such as breach of confidence which is still relied on in some cases in New York despite its rather narrow parameters, treated effectively as a quasi-fiduciary doctrine under US state law.) [59]

James Whitman argues that variations in the substantive legal protection of privacy between the US and Europe can be attributed to their different socio-cultural 'traditions'.[60] We can go further to say that diverse social-cultural traditions within the US help to explain the variations as between different US states as well. Not only are the business interests of plaintiffs and defendants quite different in California (the home of Hollywood plus now Silicon Valley) versus New York (a centre of media and advertising), but so arguably are the cultural traditions and current norms in those states. And legal context is also important. Thus, again to return to the example of California, in *Melvin v Reid*, the right to happiness in the California Constitution was a reason to support the plaintiff's claim of privacy under a tort of publication of private facts in the eyes of the court. Indeed, since 1972 the constitutional right to privacy in the California Constitution has been a source of continuing development of Californian privacy law.[61] But this cannot be the only explanation for the flurry of laws protecting privacy in the state. California is a leading initiator of data breach law,[62] biometric information privacy law (along with Illinois and Texas),[63] children's online privacy protection (offering significantly more that the federal Children's Online Privacy Protection Act, including a 'right to be forgotten' clause extending to those under 18),[64] and consumer privacy law most recently in the form of the California Consumer Privacy Act 2018 (in force from January 2020), focused on the collection and use of data online in the wake of the Cambridge Analytica scandal and citing the Constitution's elucidation of a right privacy as

---

59 See, for instance, *Chanko v American Broadcasting Co, Inc*, 27 NY 3d 46 (2016); and Brian Murchison, 'Reflections on Breach of Confidence from the US Experience' (2010) 15 *Media & Arts L Rev* 295.

60 James Q Whitman, 'The Two Western Cultures of Privacy: Dignity versus Liberty' (2004) 113 *Yale LJ* 1153.

61 J Clark Kelso, 'California's Constitutional Right to Privacy' (1992) 19 *Pepperd L Rev* 327.

62 CA Civil Code § 1798.29 and 1798.80 (California Security Breach Information Act).

63 CA Civ Code 1798.83 (California Biometric Information Privacy Act); Texas Code Ann. § 503.001 (Capture or Use of Biometric Identifier); Illinois Comp Stat § 740, 14/5 (Biometric Information Privacy Act).

64 **CA** Business & Professions Code 22580–22582 (Privacy Rights for California Minors in the Digital World).

a founding principle.[65] The protection of consumer privacy under the California Business and Professions Code (BPC),[66] and now also the California Consumer Privacy Act, both of which allow private claims, indeed goes well beyond that available under § 5 of the Federal Trade Commission Act prohibiting unfair or deceptive acts or practices in trade[67] – important as the federal provision has been for the development of a national consumer data privacy law in the hands of the Federal Trade Commission in the last few decades.[68]

But in fact there have been some notable recent privacy cases right across the US (a development that not all have applauded).[69] These include the California sex-tape case of *Michaels v Internet Entertainment Group, Inc*,[70] and the Florida sex-tape case of *Bollea v Gawker Media* (where $140 million damages were awarded by the jury for Gawker's post of a clip of 'Hulk Hogan' having sex with his best friend's wife – even after settlement at $31 million, enough to close down the website).[71] And in *Jackson v Mayweather*,[72] also in California, celebrity Floyd Mayweather, Jr's posting of a sonogram of his former girlfriend Shantal Jackson's unborn babies was held to give her a viable claim for publication of private facts (unlike his discussion of their relationship, her pregnancy and her alleged termination, which were considered to be legitimate 'public interest' free speech protected by the First Amendment). As Presiding Justice Perluss put it, Mayweather's act in posting the sonogram was *prima facie* a 'morbid and sensational' prying into Jackson's private life which 'served no legitimate public purpose, even when one includes entertainment news within the zone of protection'.[73] Further, Mayweather's suggestion that First Amendment decisions . . . preclude imposition of tort liability for publication of lawfully acquired, truthful information, no matter how

---

65 CA Civ Code § 1798.175 (California Consumer Privacy Act); California Constitution § 1.

66 CA Bus & Prof Code § 17200 ff.

67 15 US Code § 45 (Federal Trade Commission Act, 1914) § 5.

68 Federal Trade Commission, 'Protecting Consumer Privacy and Security,' <https://www.ftc.gov/news-events/media-resources/protecting-consumer-privacy-security>, and generally Chris Jay Hoofnagle, *Federal Trade Commission Privacy Law and Policy* (New York: CUP 2016).

69 See Amy Gajda, *The First Amendment Bubble: How Privacy and Paparazzi Threaten a Free Press* (Cambridge, Mass: HUP 2015).

70 *Michaels v Internet Entertainment Group, Inc*, 5 F Supp 2d 823 (CD Cal, 1998).

71 See Eriq Gardner, 'Judge Upholds Hulk Hogan's $140 Million Trial Victory Against Gawker', *Hollywood Reporter* (25 May 2016) <http://www.hollywoodreporter.com/thr-esq/judge-upholds-hulk-hogans-140-897301>.

72 *Jackson v Mayweather*, 10 Cal App 5th 1240 (2017).

73 ibid 1258.

sensitive it may be and without regard to its newsworthiness, [was] misplaced'.[74] Contrast the New York case of *Foster v Svenson*, concerning photographer Arne Svenson's 'Neighbours' exhibition of intimate images of a family surreptitiously photographed in their apartment from across the street. The New York court held this fell within the category of newsworthy and public interest publication exempted from the privacy protections of the Civil Rights Law, notwithstanding its privacy-invasive character.[75] As Justice Renwick put it, 'by publishing plaintiffs' photos as a work of art without further action toward plaintiffs, defendant's conduct, however disturbing it may be, cannot properly, under the current state of the law, be deemed so "outrageous" that it went beyond decency and the protections of Civil Rights Law §§ 50 and 51', and, although '[u]ndoubtedly, like plaintiffs, many people would be rightfully offended by the intrusive manner in which the photographs were taken in this case', it was for the legislature to address this issue, 'as we are constrained to apply the law as it exists'.[76]

Certainly, viewed overall, it seems that there is still significantly more protection of free speech in the balance with privacy across the US than in other jurisdictions, including ones that follow the US model of proliferating privacy torts. One obvious difference is that injunctions are very rarely awarded in US cases, especially against the media, being generally treated as illegitimate prior restraints with plaintiffs left to claim damages after publication.[77] Then there is the very different process of reasoning when it comes to assessing a plaintiff's 'reasonable expectation of privacy' and the 'balance' with freedom of speech. In New Zealand the Court of Appeal may have been reluctant to find the tort of publication of private facts made out successfully in a case involving photographs of the celebrity plaintiffs' infant children taken in a public playground in the 2004 case of *Hosking v Runting*,[78] but the free speech argument did not automatically prevail as newsworthy, as a US court might have found. Rather, the New Zealand court reasoned, the plaintiffs' publicity-seeking behaviour on previous occasions and the anodyne character of the images was enough to take it over the line.[79] More recently, in Canada Ontario courts have applied a publica-

---

74 ibid 1259.

75 *Foster v Svenson*, 128 AD 3d 150 (2015).

76 ibid 163, citing *inter alia Nussenzweig v diCorcia*, 38 AD 3d 339 (2007) (Tom, JP).

77 See, for instance, *Gawker Media, LLC v Bollea* 129 So 3d 1196 (2014); *Michaels v Internet Entertainment Group*, 27 Media L Rep 1097 (CD Cal, 1998).

78 *Hosking v Runting* [2005] NZLR 1.

79 See Katrine Evans, '*Hosking v Runting* Balancing Rights in a Privacy Tort' (2004) 11 *PLPR* 34.

tion of private facts tort in the revenge porn cases of *Jane Doe 464533 v ND* and *Jane Doe 72511 v Morgan*,[80] without any suggestion that free speech might prevail in the balance with privacy in these cases. (In the US, on the other hand, it remains in doubt whether revenge porn laws are constitutional under the First Amendment, as some state courts have found.)[81] Canada especially has a long tradition of strong protection of privacy versus free speech – an early example the Quebec case of *Aubry v Éditions Vice Versa*,[82] where a teenager photographed on the steps of a public building objected to publication of her image in a comment on social times in a magazine, citing her right to *la vie privée* in the Quebec Charter. In its focus on the image, the decision is comparable to the French approach to image rights under Article 9 *Code civil* invoked by Kate Middleton, Duchess of Cambridge, in her case against *Closer* magazine in Paris after it published unauthorised images of her sunbathing.[83] Such approaches seem the opposite of what one might expect in the US where the First Amendment has served as a vehicle to limit privacy in media publication cases – reflecting what several scholars have said is not just the distinct US culture of limited privacy, but also of powerful free speech.[84]

Is there a cultural explanation for the protection against intrusion on seclusion under US law, identified as a tort by Prosser (and the *Restatement*), and bolstered by the constitutional 'right to privacy' found in the prohibition on searches and seizures in the Fourth Amendment and the due process clause in the 14th Amendment? According to Whitman, these reflect an American cultural tradition of protecting the home from incursions by others and especially by the state.[85] And, although the parameters of constitutional protection have moved beyond the home and other private premises, in more

---

80 *Jane Doe 464533 v ND* (2016) ONSC 541, reversed on procedural grounds (2017) ONSC 127; *Jane Doe 72511 v Morgan* (2018) ONSC 6607. See also Yenovkian v Gulian 2019 ONSC 7279 (false light tort).

81 Contrast, for instance, *People v Austin*, SC Ill, 18 October 2919 and *State of Minnesota v Michael Anthony Casillas*, CA Minn, 23 December 2019; and see generally Andrew Koppelman, 'Revenge Pornography and First Amendment Exceptions' (2016) 65 *Emory LJ* 661.

82 *Aubry v Éditions Vice-Versa Inc* [1998] 1 SCR 591.

83 See Julie de Lassus Saint-Geniès, 'The French Tribunal of Nanterre's Enforcement of the Royal Family's Right to Privacy' (*Inforrm*, 1 December 2017) <https://inforrm.org/2017/12/01/the-french-tribunal-of-nanterres-enforcement-of-the-royal-familys-right-to-privacy-julie-de-lassus-saint-genies>.

84 See, for instance, David Anderson, 'The Failure of American Privacy Law' in Basil Markesinis (ed), *Protecting Privacy* (Oxford: OUP 1999) 139.

85 Whitman (n 60).

recent cases of electronic eavesdropping encompassing telephone boxes, cars and mobile phones,[86] the main focus is still on the home and other private premises.[87] The same goes for the tort,[88] which although now deployed in cases involving electronic eavesdropping is still largely focussed on the home (and other private places).[89] Thus although it is said that the issue is the 'type of interest involved and not the place where the invasion occurs',[90] there is little evidence in practice. On the other hand, arguably, the constitutional protection of 'privacy' in birth control and abortion cases such as *Griswold v Connecticut*[91] and *Roe v Wade*[92] represent a step towards a broader position more focussed on the sensory person. Likewise, the statement of Roberts CJ in *Carpenter* that '[a] person does not surrender all Fourth Amendment protection by venturing into the public sphere' hints at a more modern approach.[93] We can expect to see more cases testing the boundaries of the law in response to new intrusive information-collecting and monitoring technologies and practices.[94]

Again, the approach in intrusion on seclusion cases is somewhat different in other jurisdictions including Canada and New Zealand which have treated intrusion on seclusion as the basis of legal protection, loosely modelled on the US approach. In these jurisdictions there is less insistence on a narrow focus on the home (or other private premises) to overcome a potential countervailing argument about freedom of speech. Thus, although intrusion on seclusion cases *C v Holland* in New Zealand[95] and *Jones v Tsigue* in Ontario[96] involved surreptitious

---

86   *Olmstead v United States*, 277 US 438 (1928), Brandeis J dissenting; *Katz v United States* 389 US 347 (1967); *Jones* v *United States*, 132 S Ct 945 (2012); *Carpenter v United States*, 585 US– (2018); 138 S Ct 2206. See also *Lawrence v Texas*, 539 US 558 (2003).

87   See Joel R Reidenberg, 'Privacy in Public' (2014) 69 U Miami L Rev 14; Andrew Guthrie Ferguson, 'Facial Recognition and the Fourth Amendment' 21 October 2019 <https://papers.ssrn.com/sol3/Papers.cfm?abstract_id=3473423>; *United States v Moore-Bush*, 2020 WL 3249060.

88   See Eugene Volokh, 'Tort Law Versus Privacy' (2014) 114 *Colum L Rev* 879, 904.

89   For a mix, see *In Re Vizio, Inc, Consumer Privacy Litigation*, 238 F Supp 3d 1204 (2017).

90   *Evans v Detlefsen* 857 F 2d 330, 338 (1988).

91   *Griswold v Connecticut*, 81 US 479 (1965).

92   *Roe v Wade* 410 US 113 (1973).

93   *Carpenter v United States* (n 86) 2217.

94   See for instance, *In Re Vizio* (n 89) (Video Privacy Protection Act 1988 (VPPA)); *Rosenbach v Six Flags Entertainment Corp*, 2019 IL 123186 (Illinois Comp Stat § 740, 14/5 Biometric Information Privacy Act 2008 (BIPA)); *Patel v Facebook, Inc* 932 F 3d 1264 (2019) (also BIPA), cert denied 21 January 2020 – the case has since settled for $550 million.

95   *C v Holland* [2012] 3 NZLR 672.

96   *Jones v Tsige* (2012) 108 OR (3d) 241; see also *Condon v Canada*, 2018 FC 522.

photography and computer hacking in private premises, there is no suggestion that the focus need be limited to private premises. Nor does New Zealand privacy expert Nicole Moreham think it should be.[97] In *C v Holland*, Justice Whata went as far as to say that 'the tort of intrusion upon seclusion is entirely compatible with, and a logical adjunct to, the *Hosking* tort of wrongful publication of private facts. They logically attack the same underlying wrong, namely unwanted intrusion into a reasonable expectation of privacy',[98] suggesting that the tort may extend 'to searches of the person and particularly intimate searches, such as strip-searches . . ., or invasive procedures, such as DNA testing', as well as 'searches of property', including but not limited to residential property.[99] Likewise in British Columbia, the Privacy Act 1996, which creates US-style statutory torts of privacy, states with respect to the intrusion on seclusion tort that 'privacy may be violated by eavesdropping or surveillance, whether or not accomplished by trespass'.[100] At the federal constitutional level, the Canadian Supreme Court in *R v Fearon*, decided in 2014,[101] five years before *Carpenter* in the US, stated that cell phone searches in public places may constitute 'very significant intrusions of privacy'. And in *R v Jarvis* in 2019 the same court confirmed, in another surreptitious photography case this time involving a criminal prosecution for voyeurism where a teacher had used a miniature pen camera to capture intimate images of girls at school (without their knowledge), that there can be a reasonable expectation of privacy including in public places, treating privacy as including 'freedom from unwanted scrutiny, intrusion or attention'.[102]

3.3.2   The UK and its followers

In the UK much of the recent development of privacy law has been shaped by the Human Rights Act 1998,[103] bringing into UK law the European Convention on Human Rights including its Article 8 right to private life.[104] Initially, in cases such as *Douglas v Hello! Ltd* in 2000 and

---

97 NA Moreham, 'The Nature of the Privacy Interest' in NA Moreham and Sir Mark Warby (eds), *The Law of Privacy and the Media*, 3rd edn (Oxford, UK: OUP 2016) ch 2 at 42–57 and *passim*.

98 *C v Holland* (n 95) [75] (Whata J).

99 ibid [25], citing *R v Williams* [2007] 3 NZLR 207 [113].

100 Privacy Act [RSBC 1996], ch 373, s 1(4).

101 *R v Fearon* [2014] 3 SCR 621.

102 *R v Jarvis* [2019] 1 SCR 488.

103 Human Rights Act 1998 (n 26).

104 Convention for the Protection of Human Rights and Fundamental Freedoms (n 25).

Campbell v MGN Ltd in 2004,[105] UK courts depended on the equitable doctrine of breach of confidence to give practical effect to the right to privacy, identified as 'a legal principle drawn from the fundamental value of personal autonomy',[106] an aspect of human 'autonomy and dignity',[107] lying 'at the heart of liberty in the modern state'.[108] If such readings of privacy as a right became more explicit after the Human Rights Act, inspired by the Act's discourse of human rights, they could also be found in some older cases – for instance, the early Victorian case of *Prince Albert v Strange*,[109] cited by Lord Sedley in *Douglas v Hello!*,[110] with its language of a (common law) right to privacy. The difficulty was that much of the 19th century's history of the equitable doctrine of breach of confidence was later forgotten or put aside in favour of a narrower reading that was less protective of privacy.[111] By the late 19th and for much of the 20th century the doctrine was treated as largely a relational doctrine focussed on cases where information is imparted and received in confidence,[112] a distinct move away from cases such as *Prince Albert v Strange* in the mid-19th century where surreptitious or improper obtaining was considered to fall within its remit – helping to explain the argument of Warren and Brandeis in 1890 that a new tort was needed to protect privacy adequately in the face of (already then modern) incursions.

Nevertheless, a major step in refashioning the doctrine in broader terms, ten years before the Human Rights Act, came with *Attorney-General v Guardian Newspapers Ltd* in 1988 (commonly known as the *Spycatcher* case).[113] Interestingly, this was not a case about privacy (being rather concerned with the publication of sensitive government secrets in newspaper excerpts from former spy Peter Wright's book). But in a lengthy excursus, Lord Goff suggested that a duty of confidence should be understood to arise whenever 'confidential

---

105 *Douglas v Hello! Ltd* [2001] QB 967; *Campbell v MGN Ltd* [2004] 2 AC 457. See also (as to Scotland) *BC and Others v Chief Constable Police Service of Scotland* [2019] CSOH 48.

106 *Douglas v Hello!* (n 105) [126] (Sedley LJ).

107 *Campbell v MGN* (n 105) [50] (Lord Hoffmann).

108 ibid [12] (Lord Nicholls).

109 *Prince Albert v Strange* (n 27).

110 *Douglas v Hello! Ltd* (n 105) [121] (Sedley LJ).

111 See Megan Richardson, Michael Bryan, Martin Vranken and Katy Barnett, *Breach of Confidence: Social Origins and Modern Developments* (Cheltenham UK: Elgar 2012) chs 4–5; cf Tanya Aplin, Lionel Bently, Phillip Johnson and Simon Malynicz, *Gurry on Breach of Confidence: The Protection of Confidential Information*, 2nd edn (Oxford, UK: OUP 2012) ch 2.

112 See *Coco v A N Clark (Engineers) Ltd* [1969] RPC 41, 47–48 (Megarry J).

113 *Attorney-General v Guardian Newspapers Ltd (No 2)* [1990] 1 AC 109.

information comes to the knowledge of a person (the confidant) in circumstances where he has notice, or is held to have agreed, that the information is confidential, with the effect that it would be just in all the circumstances that he should be precluded from disclosing the information to others', subject to certain 'limiting principles' such as the requirement that the information should be 'confidential' (that is, not publicly known) and that protection was subject to a public interest defence balancing between the public interest in maintaining confidentiality and public interests such as freedom of speech.[114] Lord Goff confined his examples to whimsical scenarios of private papers wafted out a window or private diary dropped in the street and picked up by a passer-by. But, as Justice Laws observed in *Hellewell v Chief Constable* in 1995, the more pertinent example was someone with a telephoto lens taking a picture of another engaged in some private act, and subsequently disclosing the photograph - adding that '[i]n such a case, [subject to a defence based on the public interest] the law would protect what might reasonably be called a right of privacy'.[115]

The language of 'what might reasonably be called a right to privacy' put paid to suggestions that the UK had no right to privacy before the Human Rights Act.[116] What it had was a common law right to privacy that drew authority from its tradition deeply embedded in UK law.[117] Even before Lord Goff's influential statement in *Spycatcher*, archetypal cases of the 20th century included the 1969 case of *Argyll v Argyll*,[118] centred around a proposed publication in *The People* of marital confidences to the Duke of Argyll relating to his former wife's 'private life, personal affairs or private conduct', 'not hitherto made public property'.[119] But by the late 1980s, per Lord Goff, a further scenario being imagined was a stranger coming across a private letter or a private diary with knowledge or notice of confidentiality and then publishing or proposing to publish this, probably aided by the press. Or, per Justice Laws in *Hellewell*, photographs taken surreptitiously at a distance with a long-range lens and then published or proposed to be published in the press, or in some other media. By the early 2000s we

---

114 ibid 280–81.

115 *Hellewell v Chief Constable of Derbyshire* [1995] 1 WLR 804, 807.

116 For instance, *Kaye v Robertson* [1991] FSR 62, 66 (Glidewell LJ).

117 See Michael Tugendhat, *Liberty Intact: Human Rights in English Law* (Oxford, UK: OUP 2017) ch 10; Megan Richardson, *The Right to Privacy: Origins and Influence of a Nineteenth-Century Idea* (Cambridge, UK: CUP 2017).

118 *Argyll (Duchess) v Argyll (Duke)* [1967] Ch 302.

119 ibid 306.

also have *Douglas v Hello!*, where surreptitious wedding photographs of the carefully guarded wedding celebration of Michael Douglas and Catherine Zeta-Jones were proposed to be published in *Hello!* magazine, and *Campbell v MGN*, where surreptitious photographs published in the *Mirror* revealed Naomi Campbell (who had denied being a drug addict) attending a Narcotics Anonymous meeting in London. And, while in the first case the injunction was denied despite Lord Sedley's conclusion that the plaintiffs had 'a powerfully arguable case' (leaving the plaintiffs to a successful claim for damages),[120] and in the second damages were awarded after the fact,[121] there are other cases in which injunctions have been granted even notwithstanding the protection of free speech under the Human Rights Act.[122]

Whether this was enough to deal with all the ways that privacy may be invaded, however, increasingly came under question in the years since the Human Rights Act. For one thing, as pointed out in *PJS v News Group Newspapers Ltd*, a premise of breach of confidence is that the information must be confidential, that is, not public knowledge, and yet publication of well-known information may be highly intrusive in privacy terms.[123] Further, it is not clear that this doctrine can deal with intrusive gathering of information without actual or likely publication (although there has been some suggestion that it should logically do so).[124] Moreover, the focus of breach of confidence is largely on the treatment of information. And, as to physical and sensory privacy, the language of breach of confidence suggests there will be little emphasis on physical or sensory deprivations in privacy/breach of confidence cases. There are various torts that might also be relied on to deal with intrusive conduct impacting on physical or sensory privacy more directly in common law jurisdictions, including traditional torts such as trespass and nuisance and intentional infliction of emotional distress, as well as (in cases of repeated conduct) potentially a statutory claim for harassment.[125] However, by and large, these torts have been treated in a constrained fashion under UK law when it comes to the protection of privacy, offering little succour in cases involving,

---

120 *Douglas v Hello!* (n 105) [125] (Sedley LJ); see also *Douglas v Hello! Ltd* [2006] QB 125; *OBG v Allan* [2008] AC 1.

121 *Campbell v MGN* (n 105).

122 Human Rights Act (n 26) s 12.

123 *PJS v News Group Newspapers Ltd* [2016] AC 1081 [25]-[32] (Lord Mance); [57]-[58] (Lord Neuberger).

124 *Imerman v Tchenguiz* [2011] 2 WLR 592 [68]-[71] (Lord Neuberger).

125 Protection from Harassment Act 1997, c 40.

for instance, intrusive strip-searches of prison visitors,[126] aircraft photography high in the airspace above a property,[127]watching and photographing of people in private apartments from a platform placed on a public building next-door.[128] In addition there is the difficulty of protecting privacy under a doctrine framed in terms of 'nuisance' or 'confidentiality' and the like (for even if judges indicated that privacy was being protected this may not be clear to the outside world including those whose rights were protected). Thus, thoughtful commentators suggested that what was needed was a doctrine framed to address the problem of privacy directly,[129] taking a multifaceted view of the nature of the privacy interest.[130]

In response to these challenges, UK courts in more recent years have moved further to fashion a broad tort of 'misuse of private information' drawing directly on the right to private life in Article 8. This was a step flagged by Lord Nicholls in *Campbell v MGN*, suggesting it would offer a more direct and natural approach to the protection of the right to private life under the European Convention.[131] As also flagged there, the tort follows a two-step process of assessing, first, whether there was a reasonable expectation of privacy and, second, the balance (or proportionality) with other rights, freedoms and interests provided for under the Convention.[132] And while the initial purpose may have been more transparency in the law, the development has paved the way for UK courts to adopt a more holistic approach to the protection of privacy. The tort has been relied on to deal with numerous and diverse scenarios of breaches or proposed breaches of privacy *vis-à-vis* the UK press and media more generally. For instance, substantial damages of £60,000 were awarded to Max Mosley after *News of the World*'s

---

126 *Wainwright v Home Office* [2004] 2 AC 406.
127 *Baron Bernstein of Leigh v Skyviews & General Ltd* [1978] QB 479.
128 *Fearn v Board of Trustees of the Tate Gallery* [2020] EWCA Civ 104.
129 See, for instance, Gavin Phillipson, 'Transforming Breach of Confidence? Towards a Common Law Right of Privacy under the Human Rights Act' (2003) 66 *MLR* 726, cited by Lord Nicholls in *Campbell v MGN* (n 105) at [18].
130 See Nicole Moreham, 'The Nature of the Privacy Interest' in Mark Warby, Nicole Moreham and Iain Christie (eds), *The Law of Privacy and the Media*, 2nd edn (Oxford, UK: OUP 2011) ch 2, cited by Lord Neuberger in *PJS v News Group* (n 123) at [58]. And see further Moreham (n 97).
131 *Campbell v MGN* (n 105) [14]-[17] (Lord Nicholls).
132 See especially *McKennitt v Ash* [2008] QB 73; *Murray v Express Newspapers plc* [2009] Ch 481; *Mosley v News Group Newspapers Ltd* [2008] EMLR 20; *OBG Ltd v Allan* [2008] 1 AC 1 [255] (Lord Nicholls); *Vidal-Hall v Google Inc* [2016] QB 1003; *Weller v Associated Newspapers Ltd* [2016] 1 WLR 1541; *PJS v News Group* (n 123). And see generally N A Moreham, 'Unpacking the Reasonable Expectation of Privacy Test' (2018) 134 *LQR* 652.

scandalous publication of his sexual relations with prostitutes secretly conducted over many years (employing one prostitute to use a secret camera to film one of the sessions and then publishing the film on its website as well as featuring the story in the newspaper).[133] Substantial damages were also awarded for phone-hacking of celebrities by agents of the press following practices exposed in the Leveson Inquiry into the UK press (the subject already of several class actions).[134] Another case concerned the BBC's surveillance of the home of celebrity Cliff Richard while he was under police investigation (later dropped) for alleged paedophile offences.[135] There have been several high-profile cases about photographs of celebrities and their children in cafés and streets published in newspapers and online.[136] And *PJS v News Group Newspapers Ltd* involved publication of identification details of a celebrity whose sexual relations with other men had been widely reported with his identity revealed in overseas mainstream press as well as social media (with the injunction granted by the Supreme Court).[137] In these cases of clear even flagrant breaches of the right to privacy in its core traditional sense of a right to private life, we see judges carefully scrutinising counter-arguments as to freedom of expression under the Convention – and, and in line with the approach adopted by the European Court of Human Rights (focussed largely on the speech's contribution to 'debate of general interest to society'),[138] making it clear that they regard 'gossip' as a fairly low level form of speech in the scale of things.[139]

A second category of cases concerns data processing practices of business and government. In some recent cases there are hints that the remit of the tort may be expanding to encompass control over personal information more broadly, in line with the legislative data protection standards (in line currently with EU law standards), albeit courts still stress privacy in the core traditional sense as especially a

---

133 *Mosley v News Group* (n 132).

134 Leveson LJ, *Report into the Culture, Practices and Ethics of the Press* (Her Majesty's Stationery Office, 2012), and especially *Gulati v MGN Ltd* [2017] QB 149.

135 *Richard v BBC* [2019] Ch 169.

136 *Murray Express Newspapers* (n 132); *Weller v Associated Newspapers* (n 132).

137 *PJS v News Group* (n 123).

138 See, for instance, *Von Hannover v Germany* (2004) 40 EHRR 1 [50]; *Von Hannover v Germany* (No 2) (2012) 55 EHRR 15 (Grand Chamber) [109]; *Axel Springer AG v Germany* [2012] EMLR 15 (Grand Chamber) [42]; *Couderc v France* [2016] EMLR 19 [100]–[101].

139 See, for instance, *Richard v BBC* (n 135) [282] (Mann J); *PJS v News Group* (n 123) [24] (Lord Mance).

source of concern. An example is *Vidal Hall v Google Inc*,[140] prompted by Google's breach of the Apple Safari security system to target advertising to Apple device users where claims included both the misuse of private information tort and a statutory claim under the then Data Protection Act 1998 (implementing the EU Directive of 1995, now superseded by the General Data Protection Regulation (GDPR) and Data Protection Act 2018).[141] At first instance, Justice Tugendhat distinguished the protection of intimate private information (set out in a confidential schedule) from personal information more generally.[142] But the Court of Appeal was less clear on the distinction although generally agreeing with Justice Tugendhat that both claims could be pursued with service out of jurisdiction.[143] Again, in the 'right to be forgotten' case *NT1 and NT2 v Google LLC*,[144] claims for delisting data pointing to prior criminal convictions were based on the tort and on the statute, and NT2 (whose conviction was less serious, and prospects of reoffending less given his evident remorse) succeeded on both. In *Lloyd v Google LLC*,[145] a substantial class action following the plaintiffs' success in *Vidal Hall*, the claim was exclusively under the statute. But even here the court seemed to be searching for ways to treat the common law and statutory claims as coterminous. In response to Justice Mann's holding that the data protection claim should be struck out due to the plaintiffs' failure to detail damage as prescribed by the statute, the Court of Appeal said 'it was [not] circular to plead that the alleged infringement of the class members' data protection rights caused a loss of control over their personal data' and 'the key to these claims is the characterisation of the class members' loss as the loss of control or loss of autonomy over their personal data' – citing the right to data protection in the EU Charter of Fundamental Rights and the right to private life in the European Convention.[146] Likewise, in *Various Claimants v Wm Morrison Supermarkets plc* the Supreme Court indicated that, as to vicarious liability, the same (common law) standard applies to breach of the statute as 'to the breach of obligations

---

140 *Vidal-Hall v Google Inc* (n 132).

141 Data Protection Act 1988 (c 29), implementing Directive 95/46/EC. Cf General Data Protection Regulation (EU) 2016/679 (in force May 2018) and Data Protection Act 2018 (c 12).

142 *Vidal-Hall v Google Inc* [2014] 1 WLR 4155 [118] (Tugendhat J).

143 *Vidal-Hall v Google Inc* (n 132) [77]-[79] (Lord Dyson MR and Sharp LJ).

144 *NT1 and NT2 v Google LLC* [2019] QB 344.

145 *Lloyd v Google LLC* [2019] 1 WLR 1265; [2020] 2 WLR 484.

146 *Lloyd v Google LLC* [2020] 2 WLR 484 [40]-[45] (Sir Geoffrey Vos C). The case is currently under appeal.

arising at common law or in equity, committed by an employee who is a data controller in the course of his employment'.[147]

As to the government cases, in *TLT v Secretary of State for the Home Department*[148] claims of misuse of private information and breach of the Act succeeded after the Home Office accidentally published a list identifying individual asylum seekers online. The Court of Appeal did not elaborate a clear distinction between 'personal data' and private including biographical data for the purposes of assessing liability under the tort and statute, merely noting that the data was 'biographical in a significant sense' in this case.[149] And in *R (Bridges) v Chief Constable of the South Wales Police*,[150] involving an unsuccessful challenge to police use of facial recognition technology relying on Article 8 of the Convention and the Data Protection Act 2018 (here implementing the EU Law Enforcement Directive 2016), the court treated the practice as justified on grounds of policing and security as far as both the Act and the Convention were concerned – adding that, practically speaking, compliance with data protection principles as prescribed *inter alia* by the Act provided 'sufficient regulatory control to avoid arbitrary interferences with Article 8 rights' under the Convention.[151] On the other hand, in *R (Elgizouli) v Secretary of State for the Home Department*,[152] concerning data shared between the UK and US Governments in the context of a criminal investigation into the activities of certain alleged terrorists, the Supreme Court held that the transfer breached the Act's restrictions on transferring personal data to third countries, without feeling the need also to reference the right to privacy/private life under the Convention.

Might we expect to see a conflation of privacy and data protection standards extending to media cases in the future? So far there is little sign of this prospective development. Consider, for instance, the

---

147 *Various Claimant v Wm Morrison Supermarkets plc* [2020] 2 WLR 941 [55] (Lord Reed).

148 *TLT v Secretary of State for the Home Department* [2018] 4 WLR 101.

149 ibid [43]-[44] (Gross LJ). See also *Durant v Financial Services Authority* [2004] FSR 573 [28] (Auld LJ); *Ittihadieh v 5–11 Cheyne Gardens RTM Co Ltd* [2018] QB 256 [62]-[69] (Lewison LJ); *Rudd v Bridle* [2019] EWHC 893 [111]-[113] (Warby J).

150 *R (Bridges) v Chief Constable of the South Wales Police* [2020] 1 WLR 672 (Admin) (currently under appeal).

151 ibid [96] (Haddon-Cave LJ and Swift J); and see also the (EU) Law Enforcement Directive 2016/680.

152 *R (Elgizouli) v Secretary of State for the Home Department* [2020] 2 WLR 857.

phone-hacking surveillance class action case of *Gulati v MGN*,[153] where the misuse of private information claims succeeded in respect of the hacking and blagging conduct of the *Mirror* and other newspaper defendants. As the trial judge commented, when it came to assessing damages for 'general hacking', the figure was devised 'to reflect the fact that for a considerable period an individual's voicemail, and those of associates, were listened to and the private lives exposed'.[154] That the plaintiffs in that case did not bring claims under the data protection statute (although the media public interest defence in the Act would be of little avail) confirms the impression that this was still seen as a traditional media privacy case, involving intrusion into private life. Likewise, in 2019 proceedings initiated by Megan Markle against Associated Newspapers concerning publication of a private letter, the tort and statute (as well as copyright) are referenced and a distinction between these claims is evident in the claimant's argument that: 'The publication of the detailed contents of the Letter is an infringement of her Article 8 "*right to respect for her private life, family, home and* **correspondence**" (emphasis added), as well as an infringement of the copyright which she holds in the Letter and her data protection rights as its data subject'.[155] But we are yet to see a final judgment in this case.

In summary, for the most part still, what we see in the UK is a misuse of private information tort that closely tracks Article 8 of the Convention in its core traditional sense of a right against intrusion into private life. On the other hand, the situation can become more confused when protection is also or alternatively sought under the terms of the data protection statute where in terms of the EU Charter the focus is not just on private life (per Article 7) but also on the processing of personal data (per Article 8) – reflecting a confusion that, to some extent, also operates at the European level with its dual rights regimes. More generally, the fact that protection is being pinned to European standards indicates a certain Europeanisation of UK law on privacy and data protection, albeit there may be variations in the balance of rights and interests but still largely within the 'margin of appreciation' allowed to state jurisdictions by the European Courts. Of course, whether this will continue in quite the same shape and form after Brexit is fully in place (as far as the EU standards are concerned) remains to be seen.

---

153   *Gulati v MGN Ltd* [(n 134).
154   *Gulati v MGN Ltd* [2015] EWHC 1482 [230] (Mann J).
155   See *Duchess of Sussex v Associated Newspapers* [2020] EWHC 1058.

The question now is what these developments mean for other jurisdictions which follow the UK model but lack both the constitutional impetus of the post-war European human rights regime and the history of judicial activism of US courts and legislatures. In fact, already we have seen some important shifts in these former jurisdictions of the British world, as courts and legislatures begin to assert their powers to develop their laws, even with some very different legal and cultural settings. Especially prominent is the decision of an activist Indian Supreme Court finding a constitutional right to privacy in the rights to life and personal liberty in the Indian post-war Constitution in *Puttaswamy v Union of India*.[156] In other jurisdictions, such as South Africa and Kenya, more recent constitutions expressly provide for the right to privacy;[157] and similar rights can be found in regional human rights conventions and declarations.[158] But even without such reforms there have been some important developments. For instance, as noted earlier, in the last decade or so courts in New Zealand and Ontario have quite radically developed US-style privacy torts.[159] By contrast, Australian and Singaporean courts have so far preferred a flexible treatment of the traditional doctrine of breach of confidence to protect privacy, pointing *inter alia* to Lord Goff's statement in the UK *Spycatcher* case bolstered by Justice Laws in *Hellewell* as authorities (typically along with selected older authorities).[160] There are also suggestions they might be even more flexible in some respects than the UK courts – for instance, in their treatment of 'confidentiality' in cases where there has already been widespread publication on social media and the like.[161] At the same time, these courts have kept open their

---

156 *KS Puttaswamy v Union of India* (2017) 10 SCC 1. See also *K S Puttaswamy v Union of India* (2019) 1 SCC 1; *Navtej Singh Johar v Union of India* (2018) 10 SCC 1.

157 Constitution of the Republic of South Africa (1996), Ch 2, Art 14; Constitution of Kenya (2010), Ch 4, Art 31.

158 For instance, ASEAN Human Rights Declaration (Association of Southeast Asian Nations), 2012, Art 21; African Commission on Human and Peoples' Rights (ACHPR), Declaration of Principles of Freedom of Expression and Access to Information in Africa (2019), Principle 40.

159 See *Hosking v Runting* (n 78); *C v Holland* (n 95); *Jones v Tsige* (n 96); *Jane Doe 464533 v ND* (n 80); *Jane Doe 72511 v Morgan* (n 80); *Yenovkian v Gulian* (n 80); *Condon v Canada* (n 96).

160 *Australian Broadcasting Corporation v Lenah Game Meats Pty Ltd* (2001) 208 CLR 199; *ANB v ANC* [2015] 5 SLR 522. And see David Lindsay, 'Protection of Privacy under the General law Following *ABC v Lenah Game Meats Pty Ltd*: Where to Now' (2002) 9 *PLPR* 101; Benjamin Wong, 'Privacy and the Action for Breach of Confidence in Singapore' (2018) 22 *Media & Arts L Rev* 244; Doreen Weisenhaus, *Hong Kong Media Law: A Guide for Journalists and Media Professionals*, 2nd edn (Hong Kong: HKUP 2014) 119; Jojo YC Mo, 'In Search of a Privacy Action Against Breaches of Physical Privacy in Hong Kong' (2018) 47 *CLWR* 225.

161 *AFL v Age* (2006) 15 VR 419 [56] (Kellam J); *Wee Shuo Woon v HT SRL* [2017] 2 SLR 94 [39] ff

option to develop a new privacy tort, or torts, in an appropriate case in the future if existing doctrines do not go far enough. Another option is legislative reform.[162] The Australian Law Reform Commission has recommended a statutory tort of serious invasion of privacy for Australia in an ambitiously-named report on 'Serious Invasions of Privacy in the Digital Era' (a recommendation the Government has said it will consider).[163] Finally, there has been a steady stream of data protection laws in many jurisdictions[164] – with some commentators suggesting that, despite the motivations for these laws sometimes having more to do with economic considerations of fostering international trade with the European Union and other states than with the protection of privacy, such laws can offer real substantial privacy protection.[165]

While these are positive trends there is still the broader question whether the current combinations of laws and developing laws are enough to address the pressing problems of the digital age. As discussed in the next chapter, some different approaches may be needed entirely.

(Tay Yong Kwang JA). Contrast the distinction drawn between 'privacy' and 'confidentiality' in *PJS v News Group Newspapers* (n 123).

162 See, for instance, Richardson (n 20); Chris D L Hunt and Nikta Shirazian, 'Canada's Statutory Privacy Torts in Commonwealth Perspective' (2016) *Oxford U Comparative L Forum* 3.

163 See Australian Law Reform Commission, *Serious Invasions of Privacy in the Digital Era* (Report 123, 2014); Australian Competition and Consumer Commission, *Digital Platforms Inquiry – Final Report* (2019) ch 7; Australian Government, *Government Response and Implementation Roadmap for the Digital Platforms Inquiry* (2019) <https://treasury.gov.au/publication/p2019-41708>.

164 See generally Lee Bygrave, *Data Privacy Law: An International Perspective* (Oxford, UK: OUP 2014); UNCTAD, 'Data Protection and Privacy Legislation Worldwide' <https://unctad.org/en/Pages/DTL/STI_and_ICTs/ICT4D-Legislation/eCom-Data-Protection-Laws.aspx>;   Graham Greenleaf's Web Pages <http://www2.austlii.edu.au/~graham>.

165 See, for instance, Bygrave (n 164) ch 4; Simon Chesterman, 'After Privacy: The Rise of Facebook, the Fall of WikiLeaks, and Singapore's Personal Data Protection Act 2012' (2012) *SJLS* 391; Graham Greenleaf, *Asian Data Privacy Laws: Trade and Human Rights Perspectives* (Oxford, UK: OUP 2014).

4   Privacy law in transition

In December 2014, technology writer and *Atlantic* editor Adrienne LaFrance, summarising a recent Pew study on privacy and digital life,[1] wondered whether the very meaning of privacy will be in question when 'living a public life becomes the new default'.[2] She highlighted the comment of media studies scholar Mark Andrejevic, one of the 2,500 or so experts interviewed for the study, that '[w]e will continue to act as if we have what we once called "privacy", but we will know, on some level, that much of what we do is recorded, captured, and retrievable, and even further, that this information will provide comprehensive clues about aspects of our lives that we imagined to be somehow exempt from data collection' – in short, '[w]e are embarked, irreversibly, I suspect, upon a trajectory toward a world in which those spaces, times, and spheres of activity free from data collection and monitoring will, for all practical purposes, disappear', adding that 'I suspect that conceptions of privacy will be replaced by concerns over various forms of injustice and abuse, perhaps even over particular forms of entrenched power.'[3]

In an apparent echo of Andrejevic's words, digital technology scholar Shoshana Zuboff in her 2019 book *Surveillance Capitalism* argues that the technologies and business practices of our capitalist automated data-driven society conspire to rob us of meaningful control over our lives, adding that concepts such as privacy 'fall short in identifying and contesting the most crucial and unprecedented facts of [the] new regime'.[4] In a slightly different vein, surveillance studies scholar David

---

1 Lee Raine and Janna Anderson, *Digital Life in 2025: The Future of Privacy* (Pew, 18 December 2014) <https://www.pewresearch.org/internet/2014/12/18/future-of-privacy>.

2 Adrienne LaFrance, 'By 2025, the Definition of "Privacy" Will Have Changed', *The Atlantic* (Boston, 18 December 2014) <https://www.theatlantic.com/technology/archive/2014/12/by-2025-the-definition-of-privacy-will-have-changed/383869>.

3 Mark Andrejevic, in Raine and Anderson (n 1) 45.

4 Shoshana Zuboff, *The Age of Surveillance Capitalism: The Fight for the Future at the New Frontier of Power* (New York: PublicAffairs 2019) 14.

Lyon, in *The Culture of Surveillance*,[5] argues that older distinctions between private and public life are increasingly difficult to maintain in a world of digital surveillance, adding that the pressures come not just from technologies, businesses and state actors but also from individuals and groups acculturated to surveillance,[6] but continues to hope for the possibility of resilient norms of privacy. Of course, these are not the first debates we have had about the prospects of privacy. But they tell us a lot about the current stage of our digital transformations, when our lives can be controlled as much by machines as by the human agents behind them.

Clearly, these transformations have ramifications not only for privacy but also for law – but precisely what ramifications?

4.1   Digital transformations

The tense relationship between technology, privacy and law was evident from the beginning of the digital age. As Lessig put it in *Code and Other Laws of Cyberspace* way back in 1999 and again in 2006: 'Life in cyberspace is regulated primarily through the code of cyberspace' ('the "built environment" of social life in cyberspace').[7] That code can exert power over regulatory subjects goes a long way (according to Lessig) to explain why it 'could be a significant threat to a wide range of liberties' – controlling rather than enabling individual freedom.[8] Here Lessig seems to see only a limited role for law in responding to these technological challenges, at least in the current environment. Thus, in a 2012 *Mashable* interview he talked about 'privacy' as an 'oxymoron' in the digital age of powerful technologies backed up by powerful state and business interests. Likewise, when Andrejevic contemplated the future of privacy in 2014, he thought that all 'conceptions' of privacy would be difficult to maintain in the new digital world.[9] And countless others (especially in the early years) repeated the mantra of John

---

5 David Lyon, *The Culture of Surveillance: Watching as a Way of Life* (Cambridge, UK: Polity 2018).

6 ibid 121.

7 Lawrence Lessig, *Code and Other Laws of Cyberspace* (New York: Basic Books 1999); Lawrence Lessig, *Codev2* (New York: Basic Books, 2006) <http://codev2.cc/> 83.

8 Lessig, *Codev2* (n 7) 121.

9 See Andrejevic (n 1). See also Mark Andrejevic and Mark Burdon, 'Defining the Sensor Society' (2015) 16 *TVNM* 19; Mark Burdon, *Digital Data Collection and Information Privacy Law* (Cambridge, UK: CUP 2020).

Perry Barlow that information 'wants to be free',[10] as if law has no power to say otherwise These comments suggest that digitalisation will undermine privacy in its currently imagined meanings ranging from resistance to intrusion into private life to broader domains of personal informational control (alternatively termed 'data protection', or 'data privacy'), despite law. But in this chapter I want to suggest that the transformations of privacy in the digital age cannot just be put down to digital technologies, state power and business interests. Social norms and law also can make a difference.

That the movement might be more on the side of privacy than many have anticipated seems quite possible, as with many other social movements building up over a remarkably short period of time.[11] Already danah boyd was predicting in her response to the 2014 Pew survey that '[p]eople will be far more aware of the ways that data is being used and abused'.[12] Although she added 'I suspect that they will have just as little power over their data as they do now', I am not so sure. In 2011 boyd and Alice Marwick were pointing to the ways that native users of digital technologies across the US working in coordination were managing to maintain some control over their private lives in their social networking activities 'shaped by [participants'] interpretation of the social situation, their attitudes towards privacy and publicity, and their ability to navigate the technological and social environment'.[13] Moreover, the privacy norms themselves were evolving to accommodate the realities of the digital context. As boyd and Marwick put it, 'the networked nature of social media means that individuals' experiences with their data are constantly imbricated with others', yet they do not share 'indiscriminately' or for 'wide audiences', and being 'in public' does not always mean 'being public'.[14] In short, we have a common

---

10 John Perry Barlow, 'The Economy of Ideas' (*Wired*, 1 March 1994) <https://www.wired.com/1994/03/economy-ideas/>.

11 See Damon Centola, Joshua Becker, Devon Brackbill and Andrea Baronchelli, 'Experimental Evidence for Tipping Points in Social Convention' (2018) 360 *Science* 1116; Ed Yong, 'The Tipping Point When Minority Views Take Over', *The Atlantic* (Boston, 7 June 2018) <https://www.theatlantic.com/science/archive/2018/06/the-tipping-point-when-minority-views-take-over/562307>.

12 Andrejevic (n 1) 45.

13 danah boyd and Alice Marwick, 'Social Privacy in Networked Publics: Teens' Attitudes, Practices, and Strategies' (Oxford Internet Institute *Decade in Internet Time* Symposium, 22 September 2011).

14 Alice Marwick and danah boyd, 'Networked Privacy: How Teenagers Negotiate Context in Social Media' (2014) 16 *New Media & Soc* 1051. See also Sara Bannerman, 'Relational Privacy and the Networked Governance of the Self' (2019) 22 *Inf Commun Soc* 2187.

idea of 'social privacy'[15] – offering at the same time a foundation for social activism for real change. This seems to be what Facebook founder Mark Zuckerberg is talking about in his 2018 Facebook post 'A Privacy-Focused Vision for Social Networking', saying people 'want to connect privately in the digital equivalent of the living room', not just the 'digital equivalent of the town square', with 'private messaging, ephemeral stories, and small groups . . . by far the fastest growing areas of online communication'.[16] While we might be sceptical about Facebook's (and Zuckerberg's) commitment to building a privacy-focussed digital communications platform, this message that social networkers will search for ways to be able to combine their ideas of privacy with their social networking activities is one we can appreciate.

Certainly, in earlier periods of privacy's history there have been scenarios of markets and technologies responding in positive ways to social norms of privacy (which themselves were undergoing a process of change) – from the design of 18th century London coffee-houses allowing areas of private retreat and conversation,[17] to private communications facilitated by the postal, telegraph and telephone systems in the 19th century,[18] to buildings in early 20th century European cities catering to desires for 'independence and individuality' in the face of 'the sovereign power of society . . . [and the weight of] the external culture and technique of life', per sociologist Georg Simmel.[19] It may be that in the digital environment people will move more seamlessly between being the onstage and offstage areas of life, to revert to the language of Erving Goffmann.[20] But, as the European Court of Human Rights observed in *Von Hannover v Germany*, in 2004 (here not even talking about digital life specifically), 'there is . . . a zone of interaction of a person with others, even in a public context, which may fall within the scope of "private life"'.[21] Indeed, many of the cases from the 19th

---

15 boyd and Marwick (n 13).

16 Mark Zuckerberg, 'A Privacy-Focussed Vision for Social Networking' (Facebook, 6 March 2019) <https://www.facebook.com/notes/mark-zuckerberg/a-privacy-focused-vision-for-social-networking/10156700570096634>.

17 See Brian Cowan, 'Publicity and Privacy in the History of the British Coffeehouse' (2007) 5 *Hist Compass* 1180.

18 See Megan Richardson, *The Right to Privacy: Origins and Influence of a Nineteenth-Century Idea* (Cambridge, UK: CUP 2017).

19 Georg Simmel, 'The Metropolis and Mental Life' (1903) in Edward A Shils (transl, ed with Donald N Levine), *On Individuality and Social Forms* (Chicago, Ill: U of Chicago Press 1971) 324.

20 Erving Goffman, *The Presentation of Self in Everyday Life* (New York: Anchor 1959).

21 *Von Hannover v Germany* (2004) 40 EHRR 1 [50].

and 20th centuries discussed in earlier chapters of this book concerned not just individuals seeking a right to be 'let alone' bereft of any social connection, but people engaged in the intimate exchanges and shared experiences with friends, family and other small communities while resisting indiscriminate sharing with wider publics.[22] Or, as historian Philippe Ariès puts it neatly in the late 1980s, 'the entire history of private life comes down to a change in the forms of sociability',[23] with these changes accommodated to an extent in the architectural forms and market exchanges of daily life.

If so, one of the most challenging questions for the future of privacy will not be whether individuals and groups will desire privacy but whether their desires for privacy (however this may be conceived and understood) can continue to be supported in the digital environment. That more will be required is already clear. Urban designer and digital observer William Mitchell noted presciently in *Me++: The Cyborg Self and the Networked City* in 2003 that when the default position that the physical world allows is obscurity then those designing new systems look for ways to provide limited access (for instance, inserting doors and windows into houses), but when the default position is transparency (as in the digital environment), 'you have to work hard to produce limited zones of privacy'.[24] As Mitchell added in talking about cities of the future with Victor Chase in 2004, 'what's required are sophisticated systems that are able to control the level of public visibility' we have 'at any moment'.[25] Thus, rather than imagining a future where privacy is ceded to the power of ubiquitous technologies and practices, Mitchell's intriguing suggestion is that scope for privacy can be maintained and should be built into systems from the start – in an early powerful argument for 'privacy by design'.[26] To me, this idea of designing an environment in which privacy can continue to flourish in the future, as in the past, is very appealing. Moreover, I believe that law can play

---

22 cf Richardson (n 18) ch 5.

23 Philippe Ariès, 'Introduction' in Philippe Ariès and Georges Duby (eds), *A History of Private Life*, vol 3: *Passions of the Renaissance* (Cambridge, Mass: Belknap 1989) 9.

24 William J Mitchell, *Me++: The Cyborg Self and the Networked City* (Cambridge, Mass: MIT Press 2003).

25 Victor Chase, 'Why Buck Rogers Will Be Invisible: Interview with William J Mitchell' in *Pictures of the Future* (Spring 2004) 34 <https://www.docme.ru/doc/86920>.

26 See Ann Cavoukian, *Privacy by Design: The 7 Foundational Principles*, rev edn (January 2011) <https://www.ipc.on.ca/wp-content/uploads/resources/7foundationalprinciples.pdf>. cf F Woodrow Hartzog, *Privacy's Blueprint: The Battle to Control the Design of New Technologies* (Cambridge, Mass: HUP 2018).

a significant role here, offering a sophisticated system of its own, and working in tandem with other regulatory modalities.

In the remainder of this chapter, I consider a range of options put forward by policymakers and scholars for supporting privacy in current and future digital contexts, drawing on existing and emerging legal tools. Some of these options might have other benefits geared more specifically to 'concerns over various forms of injustice and abuse, perhaps even over particular forms of entrenched power', as Andrejevic puts it. Nevertheless, my primary goal is to explore options for the protection of privacy, whether in a core sense of freedom from intrusion into private life or in a more peripheral sense geared to maintaining a sense of identity across the board.

4.2   Legal adaptations

4.2.1   More data protection/more 'data privacy'

One option is to further expand the scope for data protection (or 'data privacy', or 'privacy' understood in the broader sense of control over personal information). Already we have the model of the EU General Data Protection Regulation (GDPR) 2016.[27] No doubt one reason for the new law was the need to give effect to the right to data protection in the EU Charter of Fundamental Rights 2000, specifying that 'data must be processed fairly for specified purposes and on the basis of the consent of the person concerned or some other legitimate basis laid down by law' and stating that '[e]veryone has the right of access to data which has been collected concerning him or her, and the right to have it rectified'.[28] But the digital environment was another powerful motivating force. As such, the GDPR represents a significant modernising step beyond the earlier Data Protection Directive of 1995.[29] Its purpose is to give data subjects in the European Union transparency and control over the way their personal data are processed, with more stringent protections for categories of 'special', or 'sensitive', data (for instance, regarding racial or ethnic origin, political opinions, religious or philosophical beliefs, sexual orientation, health, genetic or biometric

---

27 General Data Protection Regulation (EU) 2016/679 (GDPR).

28 Charter of Fundamental Rights of the European Union, 2000, Art 8.

29 Directive on the Protection of Individuals with Regard to the Processing of Personal Data 95/46/ EC.

identity).[30] It also includes specific requirements for consent,[31] independent oversight and increased penalties for breach. And there are some novel provisions, or at least ones that go further or are more elaborated than in the Directive, including:

- a 'right to be forgotten' (erasure/deletion);[32]
- a right to data portability;[33]
- a right not to be subject to a decision based solely on automated processing/profiling.[34]

When initially mooted, the GDPR was widely seen as a European tool of high regulation. Within Europe, conversely, some scholars criticised it as not going far enough even if generally their comments were favourable.[35] But by the time it came into effect in May 2018, it had a certain standing in data protection circles. Since then countries across the world have passed their own data protection/privacy laws (partly motivated by the GDPR's adequacy requirements for trade),[36] with more in train 'modelled on the new data protection standards of the GDPR'.[37]

Just how rigorous the GDPR shapes up to be depends on how it is treated by the institutions responsible for interpreting, applying and enforcing the standards. Judging by pre-GDPR cases such as the *Digital Rights Ireland* data retention case,[38] the *Google Spain* right to be forgotten case,[39] and the *Schrems* case challenging the US 'Safe Harbour',[40] a rigorous approach will be adopted by the Court of

---

30 ibid Art 9.

31 ibid Arts 7, 9 (and see 'consent' in Art 4(11)).

32 GDPR, Art 17.

33 ibid Art 20.

34 ibid Art 22.

35 See Paul de Hert and Vagelis Papakonstantinou, 'The New General Data Protection Regulation: Still a Sound System for the Protection of Individuals?' (2016) 32 *CLSR* 179.

36 Andrei Gribakov, 'Road to Adequacy: Can California Apply Under the GDPR?' (*Lawfare*, 22 April 2019) <https://www.lawfareblog.com/road-adequacy-can-california-apply-under-gdpr>.

37 Jonathan Greig, 'How More Countries Plan to Pass Stringent Privacy Laws in 2019' (*TechCrunch*, 25 June 2019) <https://www.techrepublic.com/article/how-more-countries-plan-to-pass-stringent-privacy-laws-in-2019>.

38 Case C-293/12 *Digital Rights Ireland*, 8 April 2014.

39 Case C-131/12 *Google Spain SL, Google Inc v Agencia Española de Protección de Datos (AEPD) and Mario Costeja González*, 13 May 2014.

40 Case C-498/16 *Schrems v Facebook Ireland Limited*, 25 January 2018. See also Case C-311/18 *Data Protection Commissioner v Facebook Ireland Limited, Maximillian Schrems*, 16 July 2020.

Justice. This was confirmed in the 'sensitive data' case *CG and Others v CNILL*,[41] where the Court held that Google should be treated as a data controller in respect of its obligation to respond to requests for deletion. Penalties will also likely be stepped up, as with the French data protection authority CNIL's €50 million fine for Google's failure to comply with the GDPR's rules on unambiguous consent and a valid legal basis for processing for advertising purposes in marketing Android mobile phones, in a claim brought by civil society groups None Of Your Business (NOYB) and La Quadrature du Net (LQDN).[42] But the Court also flagged a restrained approach to the application of EU data protection standards in other parts of the world in the 'worldwide right to be forgotten' case *CNIL v Google* – noting that 'the balance between the right to privacy and the protection of personal data, on the one hand, and the freedom of information of internet users, on the other, is likely to vary significantly around the world'.[43] As to the European Commission, it has also adopted a flexible position rather than insisting on strict compliance with the GDPR in negotiating adequacy decisions for trade with the European Union (although certain minimum standards such as a requirement for independent oversight, the ability to bring a private action, and special protection of sensitive data may be applied – and the Court of Justice has also made clear that these will not be the only mandatory standards).[44]

On the other hand, we are starting to see a more general move towards harmonisation on data protection standards for the digital environment and not just for purposes of compliance with EU standards. In addition to the GDPR there are other regional agreements promoting law reform around agreed common standards of data protection, including the rather basic OECD Guidelines of 1980 revised in 2013,[45]

---

41 Case C-136/17 *CJ and Others v CNIL*, 24 September 2019.

42 See 'The CNIL's Restricted Committee Imposes a Financial Penalty of 50 Million Euros Against GOOGLE LLC' (CNIL, 21 January 2019) <https://www.cnil.fr/en/cnils-restricted-com mittee-imposes-financial-penalty-50-million-euros-against-google-llc>.

43 Case C-507/17, *CNIL v Google LLC*, 24 September 2019 [60] (Grand Chamber).

44 See 'European Commission Adopts Adequacy Decision on Japan, Creating the World's Largest Area of Safe Data Flows' (EC Press Release, 23 January 2019) <https://europa.eu/rapid/press-release_IP-19-421_en.htm>; Case C-311/18 *Data Protection Commissioner v Facebook Ireland Limited, Maximillian Schrems* (n 40); and Christopher Kuner, 'The Schrems II Judgment of the Court of Justice and the Future of Data Transfer Regulation' (European Law Blog, 17 July 2020) <https://europeanlawblog.eu/2020/07/17/the-schrems-ii-judgment-of-the-court-of-justice-and-the-future-of-data-transfer-regulation/>.

45 OECD Guidelines on the Protection of Privacy and Transborder Flows of Personal Data Flows, 1980, updated 2013.

a Council of Europe Convention 108 of 1981 modernised in 2018 (CoE Convention 108+),[46] open to signature by non-European as well as European parties and endorsed by the UN Special Rapporteur as an appropriate global standard of data protection (and already being flagged as a model for adequacy compliance under the GDPR).[47] Another significant reform is the California Consumer Privacy Act (CCPA) 2018, in effect from January 2020,[48] setting new standards for consumer data protection in California (which will be taken one step further if a current ballot initiative succeeds) and shaping up as a model for some other US states and potentially ultimately federal legislation, already the subject of various proposals.[49] Premised on improving transparency and choice for California residents allowing access to their data to businesses that deal largely or predominantly in personal data, or earn in excess of US$25 million annually, the CCPA includes a qualified right of deletion for data collected from them (ie a limited right to be forgotten), and a right of data portability.[50] The CCPA may not fully match the GDPR but it provides a significant measure in support of consumer data protection while also sitting comfortably within a longer and wider US tradition of consumer protection.

Table 4.1   Rights re transparency, control, erasure, portability, automated profiling

	Transparency, control	Erasure	Portability	Automated profiling
GDPR	√	√	√	√
OECD	√	X	X	X
108+	√	√	X	√
CCPA	√	√	√	X

---

46 Council of Europe, Convention for the Protection of Individuals with regard to Automatic Processing of Personal Data, 1981, updated 2018 (Convention 108+).

47 Report of the Special Rapporteur to the United Nations, A/73/45712, October 17, 2018, recommendation 117.e.

48 CA Civ Code § 1798.100ff (California Consumer Privacy Act 2018) (CCPA).

49 See US State Comprehensive Privacy Law Comparison (IAPP Resource Center) <https://iapp.org/resources/article/state-comparison-table/>; Gregory M Kratofil, Jr, 'Federal Privacy Legislation Update: Consumer Data Privacy and Security Act of 2020' *NLR* (13 April 2020). See also Darren Abernethy, Gretchen A Ramos and Kate Black '"CCPA 2.0" Initiative Qualifies for CA General Election Ballot', *NLR* (26 June 2020) <https://www.natlawreview.com/article/ccpa-20-initiative-qualifies-ca-general-election-ballot>.

50 CCPA CA Civil Code §§ § 1798.100(d); 1798.105, 1798.130.

Will data protection/data privacy standards continue to flourish as a major technique of privacy protection in the future? If we are talking about EU-style data protection standards, expect to see some strong resistance to full harmonisation in the US especially, citing not only the First Amendment's constitutional protection of free speech,[51] but also the broad immunity from liability for the conduct of content providers allowed to digital platforms by § 230 of the Communications Decency Act 1996.[52] For despite many criticisms of the immunity's parameters,[53] this continues to be touted as a tool of internet freedom in the US.[54] And it reflects the fact that cultural differences between the US and the European Union go beyond differences in cultures of privacy and free speech,[55] and reflect also divergent attitudes to freedom of enterprise more generally.[56] So, while we might agree with Paul Schwartz that 'EU style data protection has proven to be an appealing idea' and the global diffusion of EU data protection standards 'reflects a success in the marketplace of ideas',[57] we might not want to leave it there – rather focussing in a more granular way on particular areas of convergence and divergence between the different regimes (including areas with scope for further improvement), considering new and emerging regimes which may have their own distinctive features,[58] and acknowledging the different cultural and legal traditions that lie behind the various regimes.[59]

---

51 See, for instance, Geoffrey Rosen, 'The Right to Be Forgotten' (2012) 64 *Stan L Rev Online* 88.

52 Communications Decency Act 1996, 47 USC § 230.

53 See, for instance, Danielle Citron, 'Tech Companies Get a Free Pass on Moderating Content: It's Time to Change That' (*Slate*, 16 October 2019) <https://slate.com/technology/2019/10/section-230-cda-moderation-update.html>.

54 See, for instance, 'CDA 230: The Most Important Law Protecting Internet Speech' (*Electronic Frontier Foundation*, CDA 230 issue page) <https://www.eff.org/issues/cda230>; and see generally Jeff Kosseff, *The Twenty-Six Words That Created the Internet* (Ithaca NY: Cornell UP 2019). See also Abram Brown, 'What Is Section 230 – And Why Does Trump Want To Change It?' (*Forbes*, 28 May 2020) <https://www.forbes.com/sites/abrambrown/2020/05/28/what-is-section-230-and-why-does-trump-want-to-change-it/#1dc73e10389d>.

55 James Q Whitman, 'The Two Western Cultures of Privacy: Dignity versus Liberty' (2004) 113 *Yale LJ* 1153.

56 See Franz Werro, 'The Right to Inform v. The Right to be Forgotten: A Transatlantic Clash' in Aurelia Colombi Ciacchi, Christine Godt, Peter Rott, and Leslie Jane Smith (eds), *Liability in the Third Millennium* (Baden-Baden, FRG: Nomos 2009) 285.

57 Paul M Schwartz, 'Global Data Privacy: The EU Way' (2019) 94 *NYU L Rev* 771.

58 See, for instance, Anirudh Burman and Suyash Rai, 'What Is in India's Sweeping Personal Data Protection Bill' (*Carnegie India*, 9 March 2020) <https://carnegieindia.org/2020/03/09/what-is-in-india-s-sweeping-personal-data-protection-bill-pub-80985>; Graham Greenleaf's Web Pages <http://www2.austlii.edu.au/~graham>.

59 See Anupam Chander, Margot E Kaminski, and William McGeveran, 'Catalysing Privacy Law' (2019) Georgetown Law Faculty Publications and Other Works 2190 (draft 6 February 2020).

4.2.2   More property

But data protection is not the only option being considered in canvassing the future protection of privacy. For instance, Sarah Igo notes that data sovereignty, or data ownership, is currently a popular discourse especially in the US.[60] If so, this fits with a longer discourse of property rights as a technique to achieve human ends, and adapting in response to changing technologies, as surveyed by legal historian Stuart Banner in his book *American Property*.[61] Banner starts his discussion with a reference to William Blackstone's classic statement that '[t]here is nothing which so generally strikes the imagination, and engages the affections of mankind, as the right of property',[62] *viz* 'that sole and despotic dominion which one man claims and exercises over the external things of the world, in total exclusion of the right of any other individual in the universe'.[63] But, as Banner also points out, ideas of what 'property' means and entails have developed considerably since the 18th century when Blackstone was writing. For one thing, there are many limitations on the absoluteness of property rights now recognised under law.[64] For another thing, there are other dimensions to property rights apart from the right of dominion – most notably rights of trade, including part or full alienation (moving far beyond the right of 'voluntary dereliction' of ownership and 'transfer' to another party, as Blackstone put it).[65]

At this point, we get closer to what an economist might view as the essence of a property right in personal data, established in order to promote utilitarian ends of ensuring that assets will be not only created but also exploited efficiently including through alienation. Thus, when University of Chicago economists Luigi Zingales and Guy Rolnik advocate for a property right as the vehicle for data portability in the *New York Times* in 2017, what they are advocating was a right of

60 See *Sarah* E Igo, 'Me and My Data' (2018) 48 *Hist Stud Nat Sci* 616, 622.

61 Stuart Banner, *American Property: A History of How, Why, and What we Own* (Cambridge, Mass: HUP 2011).

62 ibid 2.

63 Sir William Blackstone, *Commentaries on the Laws of England* (Clarendon Press, 1765–1769) Book 2, ch 1 [2].

64 See Sarah Worthington, 'Legal Notions of "Property" and "Ownership"', Data Ownership Rights and Controls: Reaching a Common Understanding: Discussions at a British Academy, Royal Society and techUK Seminar (London, 3 October 2018) <https://royalsociety.org/-/media/policy/projects/data-governance/data-ownership-rights-and-controls-October-2018.pdf>.

65 Blackstone (n 63) [10].

people to haggle with platforms and other service providers in digital markets in a bid to maximise their welfare.[66] Likewise, when (former) 2020 Democrat candidate Andrew Yang talked about 'data as a property right' as part of his election platform, what he was saying was that people should not only have rights of exclusion but also of 'sharing your data if you wish for the companies' benefit and your own convenience – but then you should receive a share of the economic value generated from your data', echoing an argument expressed in rather more sophisticated terms by lawyer economists Eric Posner and Glen Weyl in *Radical Markets* in 2018.[67] Similarly, when Lawrence Lessig, in the first edition of *Code* in 1999 argued for a property right in privacy he meant not just protection of personal data but potential alienation.[68]

Nevertheless, property rights in the sense of rights not just of dominion but also of trade, raise red flags for many liberal and dignitarian thinkers as well as some utilitarian thinkers. Some, like Shoshana Zuboff, may question whether, under our current capitalist conditions, property rights in personal data will necessarily result in improved social welfare for data subjects or will serve to promote the interests of those best placed to create and exploit the value derived from personal data (and data subjects), namely data capitalists.[69] Behavioural economists may point to the dangers of relying on consent as a tool of trade when it comes to personal data, given the ways that people may be manipulated, and the difficulty of valuing personal data in the current scheme of things.[70] Indeed even economists who support free markets and capitalist enterprise underpinned by trade may want to see significant reforms to the ways that markets currently work, relying on a mix of competition and data protection laws to regulate, before

---

66 Luigi Zingales and Guy Rolnik, 'A Way to Own Your Social-Media Data', *New York Times* (New York, 30 June 2017).

67 Andrew Yang, 'Data as a Property Right' Yang2020 <https://www.yang2020.com/policies/data-property-right/>; Eric A Posner and E Glen Weyl, *Radical Markets: Uprooting Capitalism and Democracy for a Just Society* (Princeton NJ: Princeton University Press 2018) ch 5. See also Andres Lombana-Bermudez, Sandra Cortesi, Christian Fieseler, Urs Gasser, Alexa Hasse, Gemma Newlands, and Sarah Wu. 'Youth and the Digital Economy: Exploring Youth Practices, Motivations, Skills, Pathways, and Value Creation', *Youth and Media*, Berkman Klein Center for Internet & Society (2020).

68 Lawrence Lessig, *Code and Other Laws of Cyberspace* (n 7) ch 11. cf Lawrence Lessig, 'Privacy as Property' (2002) 69 *Soc Res* 247.

69 See, Zuboff (n 4).

70 Alessandro Acquisti, Curtis Taylor and Liad Wagman, 'The Economics of Privacy' (2016) 54 *JEL* 442.

contemplating the exploitation of property in personal data through market-based mechanisms.[71] Dignitarian and liberal philosophers may also raise deeper concerns about whether treating data as assets ripe for exploitation creates a culture of exploitation that undermines the prospects of human dignity and flourishing.[72] These kinds of concerns about a right of alienation of effectively oneself (of selling oneself into slavery, to use the language of John Stuart Mill who argued against this extreme form of 'freedom' in the 19th century),[73] help to explain why many scholars and policy-makers have tended to be sceptical about property rights in personal data. As Sarah Igo puts it, 'probing the limits of these stories of sovereignty and ownership may clear the way for other, better stances toward the data world we now inhabit'.[74] (By way of postscript, Lessig in *Code v 2*, after negative response to his arguments for data property rights,[75] steps back from that position in favour of regulation more effectively designed to foster privacy-enhancing technologies as a less contentious means of enhancing a data subject's control over 'their' personal data.)[76]

So far, the idea of according property rights in personal data to data subjects has found little legal resonance. Certainly, as far as current laws of mainstream and especially common law jurisdictions are concerned, it is hard to find much support for data being 'technically regarded as property'.[77] Yet, there are certain well-recognised property rights in personal attributes in some jurisdictions – for instance, 'rights of publicity' in various states of the US extending to distinctive names, likenesses and other markers of identity, and protections of personal reputation under passing off laws in other common law jurisdictions,[78]

---

71 See, for instance, Australian Competition and Consumer Commission, *Digital Platform Inquiry – Final Report* (2019).

72 See Margaret Jane Radin, *Contested Commodities* (Cambridge, Mass: HUP 1996); Élodie Bertrand, '"Beyond Commodification", interview with Margaret Jane Radin' (*books&ideas*, 1 November 2018) <https://booksandideas.net/Beyond-Commodification.html>; Julie E Cohen, *Between Truth and Power: The Legal Constructions of Informational Capitalism* (New York: OUP 2019).

73 John Stuart Mill, 'On Liberty' (first published 1859) in Mary Warnock (ed), *Utilitarianism, On Liberty, Essay on Bentham* (London: Collins 1962) 126, 136.

74 Igo (n 60) 626,

75 Lessig, *Code and Other Laws of Cyberspace* (n 68) 161–62.

76 Lessig, *Codev2* (n 68) 229–32.

77 *Lloyd v Google LLC* [2020] 2 WLR 484 [46] (Sir Geoffrey Vos C).

78 See David Tan, *The Commercial Appropriation of Fame, A Cultural Analysis of the Right of Publicity and Passing Off* (Cambridge, UK: CUP 2017); Graeme B Dinwoodie and Megan Richardson, 'Publicity Right, Personality Right, or Just Confusion?' in Megan Richardson and Sam Ricketson (eds), *Research Handbook on Intellectual Property in Media and Entertainment*

as well as rights of authors in biographical works protected by way of statutory copyright.[79] Perhaps the experience of such rights might be drawn on to support a broader argument that carefully calibrated property rights in personal data may under the right conditions (for instance of personal investment, creative labour) enhance rather than restrict the freedoms of data subjects in the digital economy?

Let me give two examples of how this idea might play out in the digital context. First, in the 2009 case of *Moreno v Hanford Sentinel, Inc*,[80] Cynthia Moreno, a student at Berkeley, posted an extremely negative 'Ode to Coalinga' about her home town and its residents on her Myspace page for six days before taking it down, but then found it republished in her town's newspaper with her name attached. Moreno and her family undoubtedly suffered repercussions (including physical threats and being forced to close the family business and leave town). Moreno failed in her claim for publication of private facts, the California Court treating any privacy she might initially have enjoyed as lost by her fleeting publication. Might she have succeeded on the basis of copyright in her 'Ode'? The point was not argued in Moreno's case. But copyright claims succeeded in later cases of *Balsley v LFP, Inc*[81] and *Monge v Maya Magazines, Inc*,[82] involving the unauthorised publication of intimate images which the plaintiff had commissioned or purchased from the original photographer. And in both cases, the magazines' arguments of 'fair use' failed on the basis that the reproductions for their reading publics were not sufficiently transformative to bring the uses over the line into fair use. If *Moreno* were to be argued as a copyright case today, she might succeed on the ground of copyright where her privacy claim failed due to her fleeting publication despite the personal and indeed intimately private character of her 'Ode'.

(Cheltenham UK: Elgar 2017) ch 16; Megan Richardson and Julian Thomas, 'Image Rights and Other Unorthodox Forms of Intellectual Property' in Rochelle Cooper Dreyfuss and Elizabeth Siew-Kuan Ng (eds), *Framing Intellectual Property Law in the 21st Century: Integrating Incentives, Trade, Development, Culture, and Human Rights* (Cambridge, UK: CUP 2018) ch 6.

79 See Jonathan Griffiths, 'Lives and Works – Biography and the Law of Copyright' (2000) 20 *Leg Stud* 485.

80 *Moreno v Hanford Sentinel, Inc* 172 Cal App 4th 1125 (2009).

81 *Balsley v LFP, Inc*, 691 F3d 747 (2012). cf in the UK *RocknRoll v News Group Newspapers Ltd* [2013] EWHC 24.

82 *Monge v Maya Magazines, Inc*, 688 F3d 1164, 1177 (2012).

Second, in the class action case of *Fraley v Facebook, Inc*,[83] Facebook's sponsored stories advertising programme was challenged in a class action on the basis *inter alia* of the plaintiffs' rights of publicity under California law in relation to the use of their names and likenesses – and although privacy was not argued specifically in this case one might imagine that at least some of the class might have objected to the sponsored stories programme on the basis that their privacy was affected. Facebook sought to argue that it was merely exercising its First Amendment right of freedom of speech. But the Court's conclusion was that this was clearly a commercial advertising endeavour (supported by evidence of statements from Mark Zuckerberg and Sheryl Sandberg that endorsements from friends are worth a great deal more financially than ones from celebrities) – the case was allowed to proceed to trial in the face of Facebook's attempt to have the claims struck out, and has since settled. Celebrity plaintiffs have also objected to circulation of photographs on gossip websites with claims including right of publicity – as in *Odell Beckham Jr v Splash News and Picture Agency* (also now settled) where celebrity footballer Beckham objected to Splash's assertion of copyright in a photograph he posted on his Instagram account, citing 'the extraordinary investments Beckham has made in his image . . . [and] personal brand', which 'not only provide him with personal economic benefits but, also, allow him to drive value to important charitable causes'.[84] Whether such a claim would succeed against a media outlet, even if motivated by commercial interests is disputable (rights of publicity being usually treated as not extending to media uses).[85] But it does suggest that property rights may take on a role of supporting personal, social and cultural endeavours rather than just being money-making tools.[86]

Some scholars have critiqued some of these cases, arguing that they deal with privacy claims in the guise of property claims and go against the arguments of Warren and Brandeis that privacy should be supported

---

83 *Fraley v Facebook, Inc*, 830 F Supp 2d 785 (2011).

84 See Eriq Gardner, 'NFL Star Alleges in Lawsuit that Paparazzi Agency is Extorting Him and Other Celebrities' (*Hollywood Reporter*, 1 February 2018) <https://www.hollywoodreporter.com/thr-esq/nfl-star-alleges-lawsuit-paparazzi-agency-is-extorting-him-celebrities-1081084>.

85 See Christopher Sprigman, quoted in 'As the Number of Paparazzi v Celebrity Copyright Cases Grows, How Big of a Problem is this Really?' (*The Fashion Law*, 15 July 2019) <http://www.thefashionlaw.com/home/as-the-number-of-paparazzi-v-celebrity-copyright-cases-continues-to-grow-how-big-of-a-problem-is-this-really>.

86 See generally Jennifer Rothman, *The Right of Publicity: Privacy Reimagined for a Public World* (Cambridge Mass: HUP 2018).

by privacy torts,[87] rather than protected indirectly by claims focussed on professional and commercial interests.[88] But it can be argued that these cases are also concerned with efforts in creative self-fashioning, and indeed may go further in supporting creative productions (such as the photograph capturing Balsley's staged performance, the wedding photographs in Monge's case, and Moreno's 'Ode' to her hometown Coalinga). Likewise, it can be argued that policy makers of the future might pay more attention to the creative labour of individuals and groups involved in generating and using their personal data for 'capital-enhancing activities' – working for the empowerment of new generations of digital natives and 'particularly, those who are negatively impacted by disparities across gender, race, and social class'.[89]

4.2.3   More trust and confidence, less fraud and negligence etc

On 22 October 2019, Merriam-Webster online dictionary declared 'fiduciary' its word of the day, identifying this broadly with 'trust and confidence' and as a term still faithful to its origin: 'Latin *fidere*, which means "to trust"'.[90] But fiduciary can have a narrow (legal) as well as broader (everyday) meaning – and it is in both senses that it has become a popular expression in privacy/data protection circles. There has been much talk in recent years of the value of recognising and creating 'information fiduciaries',[91] or 'data trusts',[92] as legal vehicles for establishing and maintaining trust in the digital environment so

87 Samuel D Warren and Louis D Brandeis, 'The Right to Privacy' (1890) 4 *Harv L Rev* 193.

88 See, for instance, Pamela Samuelson, 'Protecting Privacy through Copyright Law' in Marc Rotenberg, Julia Horwitz and Jeramie Scott (eds), *Privacy in the Modern Age: The Search For Solutions* (New York and London: New Press 2015) 191; Griffiths (n 79).

89 See Lombana-Bermudez *et al* (n 67) 19.

90 'Word of the Day' (*Merriam-Webster*, 22 October 2019) ('fiduciary') <https://www.merriam-webster.com/word-of-the-day/fiduciary-2019-10-22>.

91 Jack M Balkin, 'Information Fiduciaries and the First Amendment'; (2016) 49 *UCD L Rev* 1183; Jack M Balkin and Jonathan Zittrain, 'A Grand Bargain to Make Tech Companies Trustworthy' (*The Atlantic*, 3 October 2016) <https://www.theatlantic.com/technology/archive/2016/10/information-fiduciary/502346>. But see also Lina Khan and David Pozen, 'A Skeptical View of Information Fiduciaries' (2019) 133 *Harv L Rev* 497.

92 For instance, Neil Lawrence, 'Data Trusts' (*inverseprobability.com*, 29 May 2016) <http://inverseprobability.com/2016/05/29/data-trusts#fn:origin>; Silvie Delacroix and Neil D Lawrence, 'Bottom-up Data Trusts: Disturbing the "One Size Fits All" Approach to Data Governance' (2019) *IDPL* 1; Jeremiah Lau, James Penner and Benjamin Wong, 'The Basics of Private and Public Data Trusts' (NUS Law Working Paper No 2019/019, 23 September 2019) <https://papers.ssrn.com/sol3/papers.cfm?abstract_id=3458192>; Ben McFarlane, 'Data Trusts and Defining Property' (*Property Law Blog*, 29 October 2019) <https://www.law.ox.ac.uk/research-and-subject-groups/property-law/blog/2019/10/data-trusts-and-defining-property>.

that cooperation around information sharing can be properly managed. More generally, trust in the broader sense of placing trust in the 'interactional propriety' of others is viewed as not only setting an ethical standard (of trustworthiness) but as crucial to valuable cooperation in the digital world[93] – and, it may be added, to our ability to move confidently through this world. Indeed, why limit discussions of trust to trust in humans or human-like entities when technologies may also be the subject of trust? As danah boyd says, for 'large swaths of the population in environments where tech is pervasive' there is 'no other model'.[94] On the other hand, there is also much talk of the dangers of trusting too much.[95] As Diego Gambetta puts it, 'can we trust trust?' – adding that *a priori*, 'we cannot always say whether greater trust and cooperation are in fact desirable'.[96] In some instances it might be positively undesirable. For instance, Meera Jagannathan asks, commenting on Facebook's online dating service launched in September 2019, 'should you trust Facebook with your secret crush?', given its record of breaching privacy on a regular basis.[97]

Finding ways of fostering 'good' trust in the sense of rational expectations that others will behave according to ethical norms of trustworthy behaviour has a long history – reflected in Onora O'Neill's observation that trust has been part of our law and culture for countless generations and across multiple communities.[98] It features explicitly in equitable doctrines such as breach of fiduciary duty,[99] breach of trust[100] and breach of confidence,[101] as well as doctrines framed more

---

93   Ari Ezra Waldman, *Privacy as Trust: Information Privacy for an Information Age* (New York: CUP 2018) 50. See also Sacha Molitorisz, *Net Privacy: How We Can Be Free in an Age of Surveillance* (Sydney: NewSouth 2020).

94   danah boyd, in Lee Rainnie and Janna Anderson, 'The Fate of Online Trust in the Next Decade' (*Pew*, 10 August 2017) <https://www.pewresearch.org/internet/2017/08/10/the-fate-of-online-trust-in-the-next-decade>.

95   See generally Diega Gambetta, ed, *Trust: Making and Breaking Cooperative Relations* (New York: Blackwell, 1988).

96   Diego Gambetta, 'Can We Trust Trust?' In Gambetta, ibid ch 13.

97   Meera Jagannathan, 'Should You Trust Facebook with Your Secret Crush?' (*MarketWatch*, 18 September 2019 <https://www.marketwatch.com/story/should-you-trust-facebook-with-your-secret-crush-2019-09-09>.

98   Onora O'Neill, *A Question of Trust*, BBC Reith Lectures 2002 (Cambridge, UK: CUP 2002). cf Robert Putman, *Bowling Alone: The Collapse and Revival of American Community* (New York: Simon & Schuster 2000). And see also Bart van der Sloot, *Privacy as Virtue: Moving Beyond the Individual in the Age of Big Data* (Cambridge, UK: Intersentia, 2017).

99   See Matthew Harding, 'Trust and Fiduciary Law' (2013) 33 *OJLS* 81.

100   See Lau, Penner and Wong (n 92).

101   See Megan Richardson, Michael Bryan, Martin Vranken and Katy Barnett, *Breach of Confidence:*

specifically in terms of proscribing certain types of untrustworthy behaviour, negligence, fraud and the like, which, as O'Neill says, can work to fundamentally undermine trust.[102] Even torts framed in terms of privacy typically incorporate requirements which go to misconduct, such as requirements in the US publication of private facts, false light publicity and intrusion on seclusion torts that the conduct should be 'highly offensive to a reasonable person',[103] and the UK's misuse of private information tort with its general requirement of breach of a 'reasonable expectation of privacy' which has never quite been treated as simply bolstering private expectations but incorporates some (albeit minimal and from the perspective of the subject) idea of when privacy should be respected and when it should not.[104] Moreover, reliance on these doctrines, all designed to foster – or at least not to undermine or harm specifically – ideas of trustworthy behaviour which are seen as individually as well as socially beneficial, seems to be increasing in the digital environment rather than dissipating in favour of other trends or potential trends discussed in this chapter, such as the rise in data protection and reliance on property ideas.

For example, the *Beckham* and *Fraley* cases noted earlier included claims for torts of intrusion on seclusion and publication of private facts (in *Beckham*) and unfair or deceptive acts or practices under the California Business & Professions Code 'unfair competition' law (in *Fraley*).[105] Likewise in the *Vizio* smart television case, the California unfair competition law along with the tort of intrusion on seclusion were relied on in a class action brought against the supplier of a smart television found to have surreptitiously collected user data and used and sold this for advertising purposes – and the claim has now been allowed to proceed to trial (and has since settled).[106] And a separate Federal Trade Commission investigation under § 5 of the Federal Trade Commission Act, proscribing unfair or deceptive acts or practices in trade, has been settled on terms that include a penalty and more

---

Social Origins and Modern Developments (Cheltenham, UK, Northampton, Mass: Edward Elgar Publishing 2012).

102 O'Neill (n 98) 70.

103 Restatement of the Law, Second, Torts, American Law Institute, 1977, § 652ff.

104 See Eric Barendt, '"A Reasonable Expectation of Privacy": A Coherent or Redundant Concept?' in Andrew Kenyon (ed), *Comparative Defamation and Privacy Law* (Cambridge, UK: CUP 2016) ch 6. See also N A Moreham, 'Unpacking the Reasonable Expectation of Privacy Test' (2018) 134 *LQR* 651.

105 California Business and Professions Code §§ 17200, 17203–17204.

106 See *In re Vizio, Inc, Consumer Privacy Litigation* 238 F Supp 3d 1204 (2017).

stringent notice requirements imposed on the company, providing a valuable dossier of background information for the class action.[107] A further example, also from California, follows the Cambridge Analytica scandal where personal data collected by the 'this is your digital life' quiz via a Cambridge Analytica app was sold for political advertising purposes including in the 2016 American election. The Federal Trade Commission has now completed its investigation under § 5 of the Federal Trade Commission Act, and a US$5 billion penalty was imposed, along with 'sweeping new privacy restrictions on Facebook' as part of the FTC settlement.[108] But this has not stood in the way of class actions. In a preliminary decision on a strike-out action in in the consolidated California class action proceeding, *In re Facebook, Inc, Consumer Privacy User Profile Litigation*, in September 2019,[109] Judge Chhabria allowed the plaintiffs' claims that they had 'entrusted Facebook with their sensitive information, and that Facebook failed to use reasonable care to safeguard that information, giving third parties access to it without taking any precautions to constrain that access to protect the plaintiffs' privacy, despite assurances it would do so', to proceed to trial.[110]

The case provides a striking analysis of what is essentially a 'misconduct' inquiry.[111] Specific claims ranged from torts of invasion of privacy (intrusion on seclusion, publication of private facts) to breach of contract for allowing third parties to obtain sensitive user information despite promising to protect it, deceit for tricking users about the degree to which their information could be accessed, and negligence for failing to prevent third parties from misusing sensitive information despite Facebook's duty to protect that information. In response to Facebook's argument that 'once you make information available to your friends on social media, you completely relinquish any privacy interest in that information' thus 'the users would have no right to complain that their privacy was invaded by the disclosure or misuse of their sensitive information', the judge virtually echoes boyd and Marwick's language

---

107   See Kevin Moriarty, 'VIZIO Settlement: Smart TVs should not track your shows without your O.K' (media release, 6 February 2017) <https://www.consumer.ftc.gov/blog/2017/02/vizio-settlement-smart-tvs-should-not-track-your-shows-without-your-ok>.

108   'FTC Imposes $5 Billion Penalty and Sweeping New Privacy Restrictions on Facebook' (media release, 24 July 2019) <https://www.ftc.gov/news-events/press-releases/2019/07/ftc-imposes-5-billion-penalty-sweeping-new-privacy-restrictions>.

109   *In re Facebook, Inc, Consumer Privacy User Profile Litigation* 402 F Supp 3d 767 (2019).

110   ibid 799.

111   ibid 781.

of 'social privacy'.[112] Per Judge Chhabria: 'Facebook's argument could not be more wrong. When you share sensitive information with a limited audience (especially when you've made clear that you intend your audience to be limited), you retain privacy rights and can sue someone for violating them' and 'there can be "degrees and nuances to societal recognition of our expectations of privacy: the fact that the privacy one expects in a given setting is not complete or absolute does not render the expectation unreasonable as a matter of law"' – so 'media users can have their privacy invaded if sensitive information meant only for a few dozen friends is shared more widely'.[113] The judge noted but puts aside the interesting question of whether sharing with machines is the same as sharing with humans – but notes that in any event 'plaintiffs do not allege that their information was merely subject to relatively anonymous computer analysis'.[114] On the issue of plaintiffs' harm and standing to sue, as the judge put it, '[t]he alleged injury is "concrete" largely for the reasons already discussed – if you use a company's social media platform to share sensitive information with only your friends, then you suffer a concrete injury when the company disseminates that information widely'.[115]

The plaintiffs may still ultimately lose, assuming the case goes to trial (ie, is not settled, as with so many cases against Facebook to date) – for instance, there is the outstanding issue of whether 'the plaintiffs consented to Facebook's information-sharing practices', with strong arguments on both sides (on the one side that consent in signing up to Facebook's terms was formal and real, on the other that consent was lacking despite conceding that under California law, at least prior to the CCPA, it must be assumed that 'users actually read Facebook's contractual language before clicking their acceptance', and that that 'the contract language must be assessed objectively, from the perspective of a reasonable Facebook user').[116] Nevertheless, already plaintiffs have achieved some success in the judge's recognition of several heads of claimed misconduct impacting directly or indirectly on privacy as meriting further inquiry in a full trial.[117]

---

112 See boyd and Marwick (n 13).

113 *In re Facebook, Inc, Consumer Privacy User Profile Litigation* (n 109) 776, 783.

114 ibid 798.

115 ibid 786.

116 ibid 789–90.

117 See also Pretrial Order No 26: Order Denying Motion to Certify for Interlocutory Appeal, 31 October 2019.

How would such a case be dealt with in other common law jurisdictions? For a start, plaintiffs in these jurisdictions would probably
include a claim of breach of confidence (bearing in mind that in these
jurisdictions the doctrine has far broader scope than in the US).[118] And
although there would still be the same general question of whether
users have consented to the use, it might legitimately be argued that
in a scenario of trust and confidence within the equitable jurisdiction,
courts should be prepared to look closely at the question of whether
real not just formal consent was given. Facebook might still seek to
argue that information shared on the Facebook network, even just
with selected 'friends', cannot be regarded as 'confidential'. But as
Judge Chhabria noted, sharing with some does not mean that everyone is allowed to view the information, so it might still be regarded
as relatively confidential, or secret.[119] Moreover in those jurisdictions
which have a privacy tort (or torts), a (non-US) court might go further in finding the claim (or claims) made out. For instance, if in *PJS
v News Group Newspapers Ltd* intrusive publication in the press of
the plaintiff's identity as a person who had engaged in sexual liaisons
with other men amounts to a misuse of private information in the UK
(regardless of the fact that widespread publication had already taken
place on social media),[120] likewise the sharing of private information
via the Cambridge Analytica app could arguably be a misuse of private
information.

4.3   What's left for privacy?

So what's left for privacy – and privacy law – in the digital age? Quite
a lot, it seems, whether we take the narrow traditional view of privacy
as about protection of private life or more broadly talk in terms of data
privacy as akin to data protection, or treat both as important in their
own right. Certainly, making space for the privacy of private life is still
a matter of real concern and not just for individuals and groups seeking
to claim the right to privacy as a legal right but also for legislators and
judges and other policymakers called on to translate their claims into

---

118 Brian Murchison, 'Reflections on Breach of Confidence from the US Experience' (2010) 15
    Media & Arts L Rev 295.
119 cf *AFL v Age* (2006) 15 VR 419 [56] (Kellam J); *Wee Shuo Woon v HT SRL* [2017] 2 SLR 94
    [39]–[43] (Tay Yong Kwang JA). Although see *Author of a Blog v Times Newspapers Ltd* [2009]
    EWHC 1358.
120 *PJS v News Group Newspapers Ltd* [2016] AC 1081.

law, looking to a mix of data protection standards, property rights, and doctrines more generally focussed on values such as trust, confidence, truth-telling and due care (including but not restricted to the so-called privacy torts). In recent data protection cases we see judges continuing to insist that the collection and other types of processing of personal information including information concerned with private life should be subject to real controls. Looking to constitutional and private law doctrines, as dealt with in cases, we see continuing talk of private life, even closely imbricated as it may be with public life, as worth protecting and nourishing. At the same time, a range of other concerns that take us to the perimeter and arguably beyond of 'privacy' (even in a quite extended sense of data privacy/protection) are also being addressed. In data protection law we see the beginning of a more expanded understanding of 'informational self-determination' being enacted in new or newly-expanded rights to be forgotten, of access and correction, and data portability. Rights of publicity in name and likeness, along with copyright in biographical works, fit with an idea of creative self-fashioning warranting intellectual property rights on the owner/subject's terms. And doctrines such as breach of confidence, fiduciary liability, along with duties of trustees, and laws geared to specific types of misconduct (fraud, negligence, and so on) speak to the value of trust in a civil society, especially in the current era of large distrust, with potential signification for practices imbricating the right to privacy.

If there is a final conclusion to be drawn from these trends, it is that in a time where numerous cherished values seem to be under threat from new technologies and practices there is real need for laws that speak across boundaries, dealing not only with important issues of how to maintain a sphere of private life in a networked society but also other fundamental concerns associated with the move to the digital (for instance, concerns about the effects of data practices on human identity, concerns about how human creativity will be treated, concerns about whether 'good' trust can be fostered, supported and maintained among humans in diverse situations) which equally have to do with human dignity and liberty and general well-being in the digital century.

5 Changing the paradigm

Finishing up the manuscript for this book in April 2020, things feel very different from when I first embarked on the project a year and a half ago. It can truly be said that, to adapt the language of Thomas Kuhn in *The Structure of Scientific Revolutions*, we are undergoing a change in paradigm with the scientist (and others operating in a spirit of scientific inquiry) afterwards 'work[ing] in a different world'.[1] Concerns continue to be voiced about the prospects of privacy in the face of business and government digital data practices. But they seem more nuanced than before. And the change has occurred in a remarkably short time. Even just a few months ago, a November 2019 Pew survey revealed that 81% of those in the US thought potential risks of data collection by companies about them outweighed the benefits, and 66% said the same about government data collection.[2] I doubt they would say the same now in the midst of a pandemic where collating, analysing and sharing data seems the key to survival for much of the population.[3] On the other hand, we still have the recent memory of what *Politico*'s Mark Scott described in December 2019 as 'the shine coming off much of the tech world' due to recent privacy breaches and other scandals.[4] And in the early months of 2020 there continue to be public anxieties over privacy breaches, for instance the furore over video-meeting platform Zoom's sale of data to Facebook,[5] prompt-

---

1 Thomas S Kuhn, *The Structure of Scientific Revolutions* (1962), 50th Anniv edn (Chicago, Ill: University of Chicago Press 2012) 121.

2 Brooke Auxier, Lee Rainie, Monica Anderson, Andrew Perrin, Madhu Kumar and Erica Turner, 'Americans and Privacy: Concerned, Confused and Feeling Lack of Control Over Their Personal Information' (*Pew*, 15 November 2019) <https://www.pewresearch.org/internet/2019/11/15/americans-and-privacy-concerned-confused-and-feeling-lack-of-control-over-their-personal-information>.

3 Although see Brooke Auxier, 'How Americans See Digital Privacy Issues Amid the COVID-19 Outbreak' (*Pew*, 4 May 2020) <https://www.pewresearch.org/fact-tank/2020/05/04/how-americans-see-digital-privacy-issues-amid-the-covid-19-outbreak>.

4 Mark Scott, 'In 2020, Global "Techlash" Will Move from Words to Action' (*Politico*, 30 December 2019) <https://www.politico.eu/article/tech-policy-competition-privacy-facebook-europe-techlash>.

5 Joseph Cox, 'Zoom iOS App Sends Data to Facebook Even if You Don't Have a Facebook Account'

ing attention from EU data protection commissioners,[6] a possible US Federal Trade Commission investigation,[7] as well as some early class actions instituted under the California Consumer Privacy Act 1918.[8] Yet there are also positive signs that some data companies are working hard to combine tools of surveillance with desirable protections for privacy – for instance, Google and Apple's co-venture on an application programming interface (API) designed to support individuals in COVID-19 contact tracking without disclosing identifying data such as names or locations.[9] Given that Google especially has been criticised for its treatment of privacy and personal data more broadly in the past, the development is intriguing to say the least.

Could we be witnessing the potential dawn of a new era of privacy by design/data protection by design obviating the need for legal regulation? Digital ethicist Tristan Harris (formerly of Google, now Director of the Center for Humane Technology), argues compellingly in *Wired* that technology companies are right now in a position to demonstrate 'how much good they can do when they act like public utilities operating for the greater common good, rather than optimizing for extraction and profit', adding 'these steps would mark a transformational moment, shifting the old arrangement of large technology platforms

---

(*Motherboard*, 27 March 2020) <https://www.vice.com/en_us/article/k7e599/zoom-ios-app-sends-data-to-facebook-even-if-you-dont-have-a-facebook-account>.

6 See Hannah Murphy, 'Zoom Shifts to Tackle Privacy Concerns as Regulators Circle', *Financial Times* (London, 5 April 2020).

7 See Cristiano Lima, 'Zoom's Legal Perils Mount as Democrats Call for FTC Probe' (*Politico*, 7 April 2020) <https://www.politico.com/news/2020/04/07/zoom-legal-threats-democrats-ftc-probe-173966>. See also 'FTC To Probe What User Info Zoom Collects' (*Competition Policy International*, 12 May 2020) <https://www.competitionpolicyinternational.com/ftc-to-probe-what-user-info-zoom-collects>.

8 *Cullen v Zoom Video Communications, Inc* (5:20-cv-02155, filed 30 March 2020) <https://www.courtlistener.com/recap/gov.uscourts.cand.357336/gov.uscourts.cand.357336.1.0.pdf>; *Taylor v Zoom Communications, Inc* (5:20-cv-02170, NDCal, filed 21 March 2020) <https://www.courtlistener.com/docket/17028594/taylor-v-zoom-video-communications-inc>.

9 See Jack Nicas and Daisuke Wakabayashi, 'Apple and Google Team Up to "Contact Trace" the Coronavirus', *New York Times* (New York, 10 April 2020); Tony Romm, Drew Hardwell, Elizabeth Dwoskin, Craig Timburg, 'Apple, Google Debut Major Effort to Help People Track if They've Come in Contact with Coronavirus', *Washington Post* (Washington DC, 11 April 2020); Steven J Vaughan-Nichols, 'How Apple and Google Coronavirus Contact Tracing Will Work' (*ZDNet*, 14 April 2020) <https://www.zdnet.com/article/how-apple-and-google-coronavirus-contact-tracing-will-work/?ftag=CAD-03-10abf6j>. See also Christine Fisher, 'Apple and Google's COVID-19 Contact Tracing Tech is Ready' (*engadget*, 20 May 2020) <https://www.engadget.com/apple-google-covid-19-contact-tracing-api-170057362.html>.

toward a "duty of care" that prioritizes the public interest'.[10] Others
say that, even if this might occur in response to the present crisis,
the best strategy is still to draw on the most exemplary practices in
devising regulatory standards for everyone in the future. As European
University PhD researcher Timo Seidl puts it on the *Digital Society
Blog*, regulatory action is our best hope to put the widespread experience that digital technologies might sometimes work for the common
benefit 'on a more solid and durable institutional footing', adding 'that
way, something good might come out of this crisis after all'.[11] Or, as
New Zealand Privacy Commissioner John Edwards says in a thoughtful
post, '[w]hen life returns to whatever normal means in a few weeks'
time, privacy will still be there'.[12]

5.1   The threat revisited

How different are things currently from earlier crisis moments in history which have led to institutional changes, including on the side of
privacy? Certainly, we can say that even in these times of crisis there
were yardsticks of good behaviour established through human practices and imaginations of how practices could be further improved.
For instance, the Universal Declaration of Human Rights after World
War II, with its articulated right of the individual not to be subjected
to 'arbitrary interference with his privacy, family, home or correspondence, nor to attacks upon his honour and reputation',[13] responding to
the subjections that so many people had suffered in the war. At the
same time, this identifies an appropriate standard of conduct limiting
privacy that can and should be respected even in times of war – that
is, that any deprivations of privacy should not be 'arbitrary' (already in
1948 adopting an embryonic principle of proportionality). Likewise,
there is Justice Brandeis's insistence in *Olmstead v United States* in

---

10 Tristan Harris, 'Silicon Valley, It's Your Chance to Turn the Tide on Covid-19' (*Wired*, 24
    March 2020) <https://www.wired.com/story/opinion-this-is-silicon-valleys-chance-to-step-up-
    for-humanity>.

11 Timo Seidl, 'The Techlash in Times of Corona' (*Digital Society Blog*, 6 April 2020) <https://www.
    hiig.de/en/the-techlash-in-times-of-corona>.

12 John Edwards, 'Even in Extraordinary Times, The Right to Privacy Remains' (*Spinoff*, 16 April
    2020)   <https://thespinoff.co.nz/society/16-04-2020/even-in-extraordinary-times-the-right-to-
    privacy-remains>.

13 Universal Declaration of Human Rights, United Nations General Assembly, 1948, Art 12.

1928[14] that the Fourth Amendment in the US Bill of Rights should be construed as a right to privacy prohibiting unreasonable searches and seizures by the state, taking advantage of the affordances offered by wiretapping technologies (Brandeis here adopting a position later to become the mainstream position of the US Supreme Court). As David Nimmer points out, [15] Justice Brandeis was not prepared to accept that the fact that the intrusion was in aid of 'the war against Demon Liquor' during the Probation should absolve the government of the need to engage in reasonable (ie, not arbitrary) search and seizure with a proper warrant. Quite the opposite. As he put in *Olmstead*, 'Experience should teach us to be most on our guard to protect liberty when the Government's purposes are beneficent. The greatest dangers to liberty lurk in insidious encroachment by men of zeal, well-meaning but without understanding'.[16]

Nor is there anything in Justice Brandeis's arguments to suggest that health emergencies should be treated differently from other emergencies when it comes to recognition and acknowledgment of the right to privacy. Only a decade earlier, the US was in the midst of an earlier pandemic that mysteriously arrived with the end of World War I (exacerbated by its conditions of four years of death and deprivation, overcrowding and mass movements of people) and claimed over 500,000 American lives during its dramatic spread before fizzling out in 1919.[17] As in Europe and other parts of the world, different US states experimented with infection-control measures that drew on and updated 19th-century public health practices – including closing of public places and events, personal quarantine at home for the sick and their contacts, use of placards to identify places where the sick resided, monitoring for signs of disease, disinfecting and masking practices, and isolations at the request of private physicians (including forced isolations).[18] Justice Brandeis was not immune from this experience,

---

14 *Olmstead v United States*, 277 US 438 (1928).

15 David Nimmer, 'Brandeis and Snowden', *Jewish Journal* (Los Angeles, 27 January 2016).

16 *Olmstead v United States* (n 14), 479 (Brandeis J dissenting).

17 See John M Barry, *The Great Influenza: The Epic Story of the Deadliest Plague in History* (New York: Viking, 2004).

18 See Howard Markel, Harvey B Lipman, J Alexander Navarro, Alexandra Sloan, Joseph R Michalsen, Alexandra Minna Stern and Martin S Cetron, 'Nonpharmaceutical Interventions Implemented by US Cities During the 1918–1919 Influenza Pandemic' (2007) 298 *Journal of the American Medical Association (JAMA)* 644; Francesco Aimone, 'The 1918 Influenza Epidemic in New York City: A Review of the Public Health Response' (2010) 125 *Public Health Reports* 71; Influenza Encyclopedia: The American Influenza Epidemic of 1918–1919: A Digital Encyclopedia

including in his legal life. In 1924 he authored the Supreme Court judgment in *Ziang Sung Wan v United States*,[19] where the intensive interrogation by police of a young Chinese man accused of murder of three members of the Chinese Educational Mission in Washington DC and currently suffering from Spanish Flu over seven days in January 2019 resulted in his signing a confession without proper safeguards of his rights. There was evidence *inter alia* from the chief medical officer of the jail that the confession was produced under extreme duress. As the court record summarises the evidence: 'Question. Would he be liable to sign a confession that would lead him to the gallows in that condition? Answer. I think he would, if he wanted to be left alone'.[20] Justice Brandeis concluded, '[t]he testimony given by the superintendent of police, the three detectives and the chief medical officer left no room for a contention that the statements of the defendant were, in fact, voluntary. The undisputed facts showed that compulsion was applied. As to that matter there was no issue upon which the jury could properly have been required or permitted to pass'.[21] Later, in *Whitney v California*[22] (a case in which, incidentally, the plaintiff's lawyer contracted and succumbed to Spanish Flu during the proceedings),[23] Justice Brandeis's language of 'recognising the occasional tyrannies of governing majorities, . . . free speech and assembly should be guaranteed' subject to the valid restriction that 'the particular restriction proposed is required in order to protect the State from destruction or from serious injury, political, economic or moral',[24] adding 'the necessity which is essential to a valid restriction does not exist unless speech would produce, or is intended to produce, a clear and imminent danger of some substantive evil which the State constitutionally may seek to prevent',[25] evokes memories of government closures of assemblies and restraints on free speech in the interests of public health during the

(University of Michigan Center for the History of Medicine and Michigan Publishing, University of Michigan Library) <http://www.influenzaarchive.org/about.html>; Eugenia Tognotti, 'Lessons from the History of Quarantine, from Plague to Influenza A' (2013) 19 *Historical Review* 254.

19 *Ziang Sung Wan v United States*, 266 US 1 (1924). And see Scott D Seligman, 'The Triple Homicide in D.C. That Laid the Groundwork for Americans' Right to Remain Silent' (*Smithsonianmag.com*, 30 April 2018) <https://www.smithsonianmag.com/history/1919-murder-case-gave-americans-right-remain-silent-180968916>.
20 ibid 14 (Brandeis J).
21 ibid 15–17.
22 *Whitney v California*, 274 US 357, 373 (1927) 376, 373 (Brandeis J)
23 Neil Richards, *Intellectual Privacy: Rethinking Civil Liberties in the Digital Age* (New York: OUP 2015) 29.
24 *Whitney v California* (n 22), 376 (Brandeis J concurring).
25 ibid 376.

pandemic.[26] Given Brandeis's emphasis on human rights requiring a proportionate response even in times of emergency, it is no surprise that in *Olmstead v United States* he would not accept a general argument that the government's purposes were 'beneficent'.

Of course, not all emergencies are of the same order. Yet even smaller crises can prompt new ways of acting and thinking and eventually new law, explaining much of the development of privacy law discussed in this book. For instance, in their earlier article on 'The Right to Privacy' published in the 1890 *Harvard Law Review*,[27] which prompted a century of tort law reform in the US (and served also as the intellectual groundwork of Justice Brandeis's reasoning in *Olmstead*), Samuel Warren and Louis Brandeis presented the advent of modern photography and the yellow press as a crisis requiring a new approach to the right to privacy. As such, they portended the techlash that promoted new calls for better privacy and data protection regulation in more recent years – as well as some actual reforms, such as the California Consumer Privacy Act representing a direct response to the Cambridge Analytica scandal. On the other hand, some legal changes seem to have happened in a fairly routine way, as for instance with the passing of the Human Rights Act in the UK, prompting *inter alia* a new tort of misuse of private information which has then been turned (along with data protection standards) into a legal tool to address contemporary issues. The long-gestated EU General Data Protection Regulation 2016 can be placed in the same category albeit on a much bigger scale. Indeed, quite often there is nothing that can be identified as a 'crisis', as such: rather it is just that with the benefit of experience of new technologies, practices and norms it becomes clear that new ideas are needed about how laws should be framed and applied in this environment. Or as Lawrence Lessig put it in 1999, talking about the internet's open architecture as a threat to liberty, 'we are coming to understand a new powerful regulator in cyberspace, and we don't yet understand how best to control it' – and yet the threat to liberty was '[n]ot new in the sense that no theorist has conceived of it before. Others have. But new in the sense of newly urgent'.[28] This realisation that new ways of thinking may grow over time, helps to explain Kuhn's larger comment that 'though the world does not change with a change of paradigm, the

---

26 See Barry (n 17).

27 Samuel D Warren and Louis D Brandeis, 'The Right to Privacy' (1890) 4 *Harv L Rev* 193.

28 Lawrence Lessig, *Code and Other Laws of Cyberspace* (New York: Basic Books 1999) 86. cf Lawrence Lessig, *Codev2* (New York: Basic Books, 2006) <http://codev2.cc> 121.

scientist afterward works in a different world'.[29] Or, as the philosopher Walter Benjamin put it earlier, '[i]n every era the attempt must be made anew to wrest tradition away from a conformism that is about to overpower it'.[30]

5.2   Privacy rebooted

In this time of crisis and change we might hope that even relatively well-established traditions will undergo a process of revision and renewal while maintaining some continuity with a longer past. For instance, just to name two desirable shifts that I think will be key to the future of the right to privacy in what we can expect to be an intensively digitalised, automated environment:

1.   Privacy will increasingly be acknowledged as a social good and not just as the sum of many individual goods (although the individual dimension will continue to be crucial to the future of a right that is basically founded on human dignity, liberty and flourishing). The social dimension is already evident when we consider privacy in the core traditional sense of freedom from intrusion into private life relied on, for instance, by Warren and Brandeis and still widely used today. Indeed, one of the most remarkable characteristics of a life lived increasingly online is the way that the online environment can foster and extend sharing and intimacy between individuals and groups, the kinds of 'social privacy' that danah boyd and Alice Marwick observed among digital natives in the 2010s as fostering the development of publics for the benefit of society.[31] Likewise, in terms of privacy in both this traditional and a wider more modern sense of control over personal information across the board (alternatively denoted data protection), we see that the right to privacy may not just be valuable in its

---

29 Kuhn (n 1).

30 Walter Benjamin, 'Theses on the Philosophy of History' (1940) in Hannah Arendt (ed), transl Harry Zohn, *Illuminations* (New York: Harcourt, Brace & World, 1968) 255, 257.

31 danah boyd and Alice Marwick, 'Social Privacy in Networked Publics: Teens' Attitudes, Practices, and Strategies' (Oxford Internet Institute *Decade in Internet Time* Symposium, 22 September, 2011); Alice Marwick and danah boyd, 'Networked Privacy: How Teenagers Negotiate Context in Social Media' (2014) 16 New Media & Soc 1051. And see Mark Carrigan, 'Will Covid-19 Generate an Epidemiological Folk Consciousness? What Will this Mean for Platform Capitalism?' (markcarrigan.net, 12 April 2020) <https://markcarrigan.net/2020/04/12/will-covid-19-generate-an-epidemiological-folk-consciousness-what-will-this-mean-for-platform-capitalism>.

own terms but as an enabling right promoting a range of socially beneficial outcomes such as freedom of speech and political participation in democratic institutions.[32] Likewise, in debates about surveillance technologies adopted to assist in controlling the current pandemic, warnings about the need for attention to be paid to maintaining privacy/data protection standards are expressed as serious concerns not just involving particular data subjects but the entire public health effort depending as it does on levels of community trust.[33] In a similar vein, philosopher Yuval Noah Harari argues vigorously that privacy, freedom and democracy and will be lost irrevocably if emergency laws allowing uncontrolled tracking and monitoring are adopted to deal with a pandemic and then continue in place, especially in a world in which 'for the first time in human history, technology makes it possible to monitor everyone all the time'.[34] At the same time, the EU Data Protection Board's prescript that 'these apps are not social platforms for spreading social alarm or giving rise to any sort of stigmatisation',[35] can be applied more broadly – setting a standard not just for state monitoring but equally dangerous untrammelled social monitoring of individuals and groups.[36] Finally, in this time of pandemic, we might hope for some new ways of thinking about the social value of private life within the physical walls of the home, allowing opportunities for quiet reflection,

---

32 As noted, for instance, by Ben Goold, 'Surveillance and the Political Value of Privacy' (2009) ALF 3; Neil Richards, *Intellectual Privacy: Rethinking Civil Liberties in the Digital Age* (New York: OUP 2015); Andrew Roberts, 'A Republican Account of the Value of Privacy' (2015) 14 Eur J Pol Theor 320; Manon Oostveen and Kristina Irion, 'The Golden Age of Personal Data: How to Regulate an Enabling Fundamental Right?' in Mor Bakhoum, Beatriz Conde Gallego, Mark-Oliver Mackenrodt, Gintarė Surblytė-Namavičienė (eds), *Personal Data in Competition, Consumer Protection and IP Law: Towards a Holistic Approach?* (Berlin: Springer 2018) 7.

33 See, for instance, Carmela Troncoso et al, 'Decentralised Privacy-Preserving Proximity Tracing (DP-PPT): White Paper' (*GitHub*, 12 April 2020) <https://github.com/DP-3T/documents/blob/master/DP3T%20White%20Paper.pdf>; Vanessa Teague, 'Contact Tracing without Surveillance' (*GitHub*, 14 April 2020; <https://github.com/vteague/contactTracing>; Michelle M Mello and C Jason Wang, 'Ethics and Governance for Digital Disease Surveillance' (2020) 368 *Science* 951 <https://science.sciencemag.org/content/368/6494/951>. See also Jake Goldenfein, Ben Green and Salomé Viljoen, 'Privacy Versus Health Is a False Trade-Off' (*Jacobin*, 17 April 2020) <https://jacobinmag.com/2020/04/privacy-health-surveillance-coronavirus-pandemic-technology>.

34 Yuval Noah Harari, 'The World After Coronavirus', *Financial Times* (London, 20 March 2020).

35 EDPB Letter Concerning the European Commission's draft Guidance on Apps Supporting the Fight against the COVID-19 Pandemic (14 April 2020) <https://edpb.europa.eu/sites/edpb/files/files/file1/edpbletterecadvisecodiv-appguidance_final.pdf>.

36 Recalling David Lyon, *The Culture of Surveillance: Watching as a Way of Life* (Cambridge, UK: Polity 2018).

fresh insight and creativity – but also, with the benefit of digital technologies and communications, leading to new forms of socially valuable cultural exchange.[37]

2. The idea of a 'right to privacy' will become even more widely accepted and will also spawn a range of contiguous rights which may ultimately take on lives of their own. Already, we are seeing rights identified under the banner of the right to privacy which are only debatably to do with privacy – at least, in the traditional sense of a right to the privacy of private life, and even arguably in the more modern sense of control over personal information (alternatively encapsulated in the European language of data protection). But clearly these rights have to do with maintaining a sense of identity, in the face of what Shoshana Zuboff and others have identified as concerted efforts to exercise power over us by leveraging our data.[38] These include such rights as the right to be forgotten (or erasure), the right to data portability, and the right not to be subject to a decision based solely on automated profiling recognised in the GDPR and to an extent the CCPA (at least regarding the first two rights) and in various degrees in other current laws.[39] Indeed, it is hard to believe that only a few years ago there was little need seen for the third right,[40] the second had been hardly thought of in privacy and data protection circles,[41] and the first was criticised by a prominent US privacy scholar as 'the biggest threat to free speech on the Internet in the coming decade'.[42] We can expect to see the trend of identifying new kinds of rights continue in newer laws (including some still to be framed).[43] In general, they fit a pattern of modern regimes

---

37 See 'Young Artists Examine Life In The Time Of COVID-19' <https://www.fya.org.au/2020/03/31/young-artists-examine-life-in-the-time-of-covid-19>.

38 Shoshana Zuboff, *The Age of Surveillance Capitalism: The Fight for the Future at the New Frontier of Power* (New York: PublicAffairs 2019); cf Harari (n 34).

39 GDPR, Arts 17, 20, 22; CCPA CA Civil Code, §§ 1798.105, 1798.130; Council of Europe, Convention for the Protection of Individuals with regard to Automatic Processing of Personal Data, 1981, updated 2018 (Convention 108+), Arts 9(1)(a) and (e).

40 Although see presciently Mireille Hildebrandt and Bert-Jaap Koops, The Challenges of Ambient Law and Legal Protection in the Profiling Era (2010) 73 *MLR* 428.

41 Although see also presciently Viktor Mayer-Schönberger, *Delete: The Virtue of Forgetting in the Digital Age* (Dordrecht: Springer 2010).

42 Geoffrey Rosen, 'The Right to Be Forgotten' (2012) 64 *Stan L Rev Online* 88.

43 See, for instance, Arindrajit Basu and Justin Sherman, 'Key Global Takeaways From India's Revised Personal Data Protection Bill' (*Lawfare*, 23 January 2020) <https://www.lawfareblog.com/key-global-takeaways-indias-revised-personal-data-protection-bill>; Anirudh Burman and Suyash Rai, 'What Is in India's Sweeping Personal Data Protection Bill' (*Carnegie India*, 9 March 2020)

providing an array of rights and duties that protect heterogene-
ous dimensions of human identity in circumstances that take us
beyond, or at least to the margins of, traditional 'privacy' and even
'data privacy' as we have more lately come to know it.

In this short book I have been stressing that an understanding of how
traditions become established and change over time and space is crucial in thinking about transformations of privacy and the institutions
that surround and support it (recalling the insights of Ferdinand de
Saussure over a century ago).[44] As digital humanities scholar Kathleen
Fitzpatrick puts it neatly,[45] considering rather ironically the tradition
of the book as a source of knowledge, 'processes of establishing conventions, and making them conventional, [are] . . . the product of social
negotiations involving a wide range of actors'. And the question now is
not just whether the right to privacy will continue in the face of all the
great challenges we are facing but whether – and how - it will continue
to respond to the most pressing human needs of the future.

5.3   Finale

10 December 2019 might seem a world away from April 2020, given all
that has happened in the intervening months. Nevertheless, I remem-
ber it quite distinctly. I was involved in a panel discussion on the right
to privacy at the Wheeler Centre in Melbourne, a self-described 'home
for smart, passionate and entertaining public talks on every topic'.[46] Just
a few days earlier I had been listening to a range of fascinating papers
from knowledgeable and engaged scholars talking about the state of
privacy and law in the region at the Asian Privacy Scholars Network
Conference in Singapore. It was Human Rights Day, commemorating
the United Nation's adoption of the Universal Declaration of Human
Rights on 10 December 1948.[47] Sitting there on the Wheeler Centre

---

<https://carnegieindia.org/2020/03/09/what-is-in-india-s-sweeping-personal-data-protection-bill-pub-80985>.

44 Ferdinand de Saussure, *Course in General Linguistics*, Charles Bally and Albert Sechehaye with Albert Reidlinger (eds) (⊠first published Paris: Payot 1916, Wade Baskin tr, London: Peter Owen 1960).

45 Kathleen Fitzpatrick, 'The Future History of the Book: Time, Attention, Convention' in Babette B Tischleder and Sarah Wasserman (eds), *Cultures of Obsolescence* (New York: Palgrave 2015) 111, 122.

46 The Wheeler Centre <https://www.wheelercentre.com>.

47 The Universal Declaration of Human Rights, United Nations General Assembly, 1948, Art 12.

stage reflecting on the state of privacy and privacy law in Australia and the world, and comparing notes with my fellow-panelists, human rights lawyer Lizzie O'Shea, author of *Future Histories*,[48] and the redoubtable Victorian Information Commissioner Sven Bluemmel, I realized that I felt quite pleased about the shift in paradigm with privacy now starting to be seen as something that should be taken seriously by policymakers – as well as by people more generally.

Indeed, looking forward now a few months into 2020, even with all that has occurred and plenty more to look forward to before we can find a 'new normal' after our major terrifying pandemic finally dissipates, there is a real sense that the right to privacy is something that needs to be treated with respect. Of course, there is still a lot to contend with – I suspect that privacy could easily end up being a rare commodity that used to be plentiful (at least for rich people in the rich world), in the way of water, clean air, food safety, health, and green environment. Or as Bob Mankoff of the *New Yorker* predicted in 1997, privacy will become like the 15 minutes of fame we used to crave when fame was rare.[49] But we can nevertheless appreciate its value and work hard to preserve it even if this means making tradeoffs for other goods that may also contribute to human dignity, liberty and general wellbeing. We might not deal all that well with the threats now and emerging. But there are exciting times ahead as policymakers start trying!

---

48 Lizzie O'Shea, *Future Histories: What Ada Lovelace, Tom Paine, and the Paris Commune Can Teach Us about Digital Technology* (London, New York: Verso 2019).

49 Bob Mankoff, 'In the Future, Everyone Will Have Privacy For Fifteen Minutes' *New Yorker* (December 1997). See Bob Mankoff, 'Selfie Explanatorie' <https://www.newyorker.com/cartoons/bob-mankoff/selfie-explanatorie>.

Select bibliography

Acquisti, Alessandro; Taylor, Curtis; and Wagman, Liad, 'The Economics of Privacy' (2016) 54 *JEL* 442.

Allen, A, 'Taking Liberties: Privacy, Private Choice, and Social Contract Theory' (1987) 56 *U Cin L Rev* 561.

Allen, Anita, *Unpopular Privacy: What Must We Hide?* (New York: Oxford 2017).

Andrejevic, Mark, *Automated Media* (New York: Routledge 2020).

Andrejevic, Mark, and Burdon, Mark, 'Defining the Sensor Society' (2015) 16 *TVNM* 19.

Aplin, Tanya; Bently, Lionel; Johnson, Phillip; and Malynicz, Simon, *Gurry on Breach of Confidence: The Protection of Confidential Information* (Oxford, UK: OUP 2012).

Ariès, Philippe, and Duby, Georges (eds), *A History of Private Life*, vol 3: *Passions of the Renaissance* (Cambridge, Mass: Belknap 1989).

Austin, Lisa, 'Privacy and the Question of Technology' (2003) 22 *Law & Phil* 119.

Balkin, Jack M, 'Information Fiduciaries and the First Amendment'; (2016) 49 *UCD L Rev* 1183.

Bannerman, Sara, 'Relational Privacy and the Networked Governance of the Self' (2019) 22 *Inf Commun Soc* 2187.

Bakhoum, Mor; Gallego, Beatriz Conde; Mackenrodt, Mark-Oliver; Surblytė-Namavičienė, Gintarė (eds), *Personal Data in Competition, Consumer Protection and IP Law: Towards a Holistic Approach?* (Berlin: Springer 2018).

boyd, danah, and Marwick, Alice, 'Social Privacy in Networked Publics: Teens' Attitudes, Practices, and Strategies' (Oxford Internet Institute *Decade in Internet Time* Symposium, 22 September 2011).

Bridges, Khiara, *The Poverty of Privacy Rights* (Stanford, Cal: SUP 2017).

Burdon, Mark, *Digital Data Collection and Information Privacy Law* (Cambridge, UK: CUP 2020).

Bygrave, Lee, *Data Privacy Law: An International Perspective* (Oxford, UK: OUP 2014).

Chander, Anupam; Kaminski, Margot E; and McGeveran, William, 'Catalysing Privacy Law' (2019) *Georgetown Law Faculty Publications and Other Works* 2190.

Chesterman, Simon, 'After Privacy: The Rise of Facebook, the Fall of WikiLeaks, and Singapore's Personal Data Protection Act 2012' (2012*) SJLS* 391.

Ciacchi, Aurelia Colombi; Godt, Christine; Rott, Peter; and Smith, Leslie Jane (eds), *Liability in the Third Millennium* (Baden-Baden, FRG: Nomos 2009).

Cohen, Julie E, *Configuring the Networked Self* (New Haven, Conn: YUP 2012).

Cohen, Julie E, *Between Truth and Power: The Legal Constructions of Informational Capitalism* (New York: OUP 2019).

de Hert, Paul, and Papakonstantinou, Vagelis, 'The New General Data Protection Regulation: Still a Sound System for the Protection of Individuals?' (2016) 32 *CLSR* 179.

Fried, Charles, 'Privacy' (1968) 77 *Yale LJ* 475.

Gavison, Ruth, 'Privacy and the Limits of Law' (1980) 89 *Yale LJ* 421.

Goldenfein, Jake, *Monitoring Laws: Profiling and Identity in the World State* (New York: CUP 2020).

Goold, Ben, 'Surveillance and the Political Value of Privacy' (2009) *ALF* 3.

Greenleaf, Graham, *Asian Data Privacy Laws: Trade and Human Rights Perspectives* (Oxford, UK: OUP 2014).

Gutwirth, Serge; Poullet, Yves; De Hert, Paul; de Terwangne, Cécile; and Nouwt, Sjaak (eds), *Reinventing Data Protection?* (Dordrecht: Springer 2009).

Harari, Yuval Noah, *Homo Deus: A Brief History of Tomorrow* (New York: HarperCollins 2017) 322.

Hildebrandt, Mireille, and Koops, Bert-Jaap, 'The Challenges of Ambient Law and Legal Protection in the Profiling Era' (2010) 73 *MLR* 428.

Hughes, Kirsty, 'A Behavioural Understanding of Privacy and its Implications for Privacy Law' (2012) 75 *MLR* 806.

Igo, Sarah E, 'Me and My Data' (2018) 48 *Hist Stud Nat Sci* 616.

Igo, Sarah E, *The Known Citizen: A History of Privacy in Modern America* (Cambridge, Mass: HUP 2018).

Kenyon, Andrew T (ed), *Comparative Defamation and Privacy Law* (Cambridge, UK: CUP 2016).

Khan, Lina, and Pozen, David, 'A Skeptical View of Information Fiduciaries' (2019) 133 *Harv L Rev* 497.

Koops, Bert-Jaap; Newell, Bryce Clayton; Timan, Tjerk; Skorvánek, Ivan; Chokrevski, Tomislav; and Galič, Maša, 'A Typology of Privacy' (2017) 38 *UPJIL* 483.

Lake, Jessica, *The Face that Launched a Thousand Lawsuits: The American Women Who Forged a Right to Privacy* (New Haven, Conn: YUP 2016).

Lessig, Lawrence, *Code and Other Laws of Cyberspace* (New York: Basic Books 1999).

Lessig, Lawrence, *Code*v2 (New York: Basic Books 2006).

Lynskey, Orla, 'Deconstructing Data Protection: the "Added-Value" of a Right to Data Protection in the EU Legal Order' (2014) 63 *ICLQ* 569.

Lyon, David, *The Culture of Surveillance: Watching as a Way of Life* (Cambridge, UK: Polity 2018).

Madden, Mary; Gilman, Michele; Levy, Karen; and Marwick, Alice, 'Privacy, Poverty, and Big Data: A Matrix of Vulnerabilities for Poor Americans' (2017) 95 *Wash U L Rev* 53.

Marwick, Alice, and boyd, danah, 'Networked Privacy: How Teenagers Negotiate Context in Social Media' (2014) 16 *New Media & Soc* 1051.

Mayer-Schönberger, Viktor, *Delete: The Virtue of Forgetting in the Digital Age* (Dordrecht: Springer 2010).

Molitorisz, Sacha, *Net Privacy: How We Can Be Free in an Age of Surveillance* (Sydney: NewSouth 2020)

Monti, Andrea, and Wacks, Raymond, *The Right to Privacy Reconsidered* (Oxford, UK: Hart 2019).

Moreham, NA, and Warby, Sir Mark (Sir Michael Tugendhat and Iain Christie consultant eds), *Tugendhat and Christie: The Law of Privacy and the Media*, 3rd edn (Oxford, UK: OUP 2016).

Moreham, NA, 'Unpacking the Reasonable Expectation of Privacy Test' (2018) 134 *LQR* 652.

Nissenbaum, Helen, *Privacy in Context: Technology, Policy and the Integrity of Social Life* (Stanford, Cal: SUP 2010).

O'Neill, Onora, *A Question of Trust*, BBC Reith Lectures 2002 (Cambridge, UK: CUP 2002).

O'Shea, Lizzie, *Future Histories: What Ada Lovelace, Tom Paine, and the Paris Commune Can Teach Us about Digital Technology* (London/New York: Verso 2019).

Posner, Eric A, and Weyl, E Glen, *Radical Markets: Uprooting Capitalism and Democracy for a Just Society* (Princeton NJ: Princeton University Press 2018).

Richards, Neil, *Intellectual Privacy: Rethinking Civil Liberties in the Digital Age* (New York: OUP 2015).

Richards, Neil, 'The Dangers of Surveillance' (2013) 126 *Harv L Rev* 1934.

Richardson, Megan; Bryan, Michael; Vranken, Martin; and Barnett, Katy, *Breach of Confidence: Social Origins and Modern Developments* (Cheltenham, UK, Northampton, Mass: Edward Elgar Publishing 2012).

Richardson, Megan, *The Right to Privacy: Origins and Influence of a Nineteenth-Century Idea* (Cambridge, UK: CUP 2017).

Roberts, Andrew, 'A Republican Account of the Value of Privacy' (2015) 14 *Eur J Pol Theor* 320.

Roessler, Beate, 'Privacy as a Human Right' (2017) 117 *Proc Aristot Soc* 187.

Rosen, Geoffrey, 'The Right to Be Forgotten' (2012) 64 *Stan L Rev Online* 88.

Rössler, Beate, *The Value of Privacy*, Rupert Glasgow (tr) (Oxford: Polity 2005).

Rotenberg, Marc; Horwitz, Julia; and Scott, Jeramie (eds), *Privacy in the Modern Age: The Search For Solutions* (New York and London: New Press 2015).

Rothman, Jennifer, *The Right of Publicity: Privacy Reimagined for a Public World* (Cambridge, Mass: HUP 2018).

Schwartz, Paul M, 'Global Data Privacy: The EU Way' (2019) 94 *NYU L Rev* 771.

Solove, Daniel K, *Understanding Privacy* (Cambridge, Mass: HUP 2008).

Solove, Daniel J, and Schwartz, Paul M, *Information Privacy Law*, 6th edn (Frederick, Md: Wolters Kluwer 2017).

Tugendhat, Michael, *Liberty Intact: Human Rights in English Law* (Oxford, UK: OUP 2017).

van der Sloot, Bart, *Privacy as Virtue: Moving Beyond the Individual in the Age of Big Data* (Cambridge, UK: Intersentia 2017).

Vismann, Cornelia, *Files: Law and Media Technology*, Geoffrey Winthrop-Young (tr) (Stanford, Cal: SUP 2008).

Waldman, Ari Ezra *Privacy as Trust: Information Privacy for an Information Age* (New York: CUP 2018).

Warren, Samuel D, and Brandeis, Louis D, 'The Right to Privacy' (1890) 4 *Harv L Rev* 193.

Westin, Alan F, *Privacy and Freedom* (New York: Atheneum 1967).

Whitman, James Q, 'The Two Western Cultures of Privacy: Dignity Versus Liberty' (2004) 113 *Yale LJ* 1151.

Zuboff, Shoshana, *The Age of Surveillance Capitalism: The Fight for the Future at the New Frontier of Power* (New York: PublicAffairs 2019).

Index

95

Titles in the **Elgar Advanced Introductions** series include: